# WHAT EVERYONE
# NEEDS TO KNOW
# ABOUT ISLAM

# What Everyone Needs to Know About

# Islam

## JOHN L. ESPOSITO

OXFORD
UNIVERSITY PRESS

2002

# OXFORD

UNIVERSITY PRESS

Oxford   New York
Auckland   Bangkok   Buenos Aires   Cape Town   Chennai
Dar es Salaam   Delhi   Hong Kong   Istanbul   Karachi   Kolkata
Kuala Lumpur   Madrid   Melbourne   Mexico City   Mumbai   Nairobi
São Paulo   Shanghai   Singapore   Taipei   Tokyo   Toronto

Published by Oxford University Press, Inc.
198 Madison Avenue, New York, New York, 10016

www.oup.com

Oxford is a registered trademark of Oxford University Press

**Library of Congress Cataloging-in-Publication Data**
Esposito, John L.
What everyone needs to know about Islam / John L. Esposito.
p.   cm.
Includes bibliographical references.
ISBN-13 978-0-19-515713-0

1. Islam—Essence, genius, nature. I. Title
BP163.E85   2002
297—dc21   2002008387

11

Printed in the United States of America
on acid-free paper

*For Jean,*
*Who Makes All Things Possible*

# CONTENTS

## *Islam and Other Religions*

## *Customs and Culture*

## *Violence and Terrorism*

# Society, Politics, and Economy

# Muslims in the West

# PREFACE

This brief volume grows out of my experiences after the tragedy of 9/11. Like many of my colleagues, I have been bombarded with questions about Islam and Muslims. So many are now trying to understand "why" and "how." While some questions center on the attacks against the World Trade Center and the Pentagon, many are the same queries that have arisen time and again over the years in media interviews, government and corporate briefings, and presentations at universities and civic organizations: Why is Islam so violent? Does the Quran approve terrorism and suicide bombing? Is Islam compatible with modernity? Why do Muslims persecute Jews and Christians?

Reflecting on 9/11 and these persistent questions, I realized how much has changed and how much remains the same. Islam is the second largest of the world's religions globally as well as in Europe, and it is the third largest religion in America. Yet many in the West continue to function within an enormous information vacuum, the same one I myself suffered from over thirty years ago. When I first encountered Islam in graduate school, I was astonished to discover that there was another Abrahamic faith. We had always talked about the Judeo-Christian connection, but never the Judeo-Christian-Islamic tradition. Why? If Muslims recognize and revere many of the major patriarchs and prophets of Judaism and Christianity (including Abraham, Moses, and Jesus) and God's revealed books, the

Torah and the Message (Gospels) of Jesus, why had I not been aware of this after all my years of liberal arts and theological training?

Learning about Islam gave me a new perspective, a new way of understanding history, from the Crusades and European colonialism to American and Soviet neocolonialism. Thus not only religion but also history, politics, and civilization, classical and modern, came alive for me. Today, however, many are still relying on media stereotypes, seeing Islam through distorted lenses that focus on terrorists, religious extremists, and oppressed women. The actions of a radicalized minority become equated with the faith of the mainstream majority. And yet Muslims are now an integral part of the religious landscape of America and Europe; they are increasingly our fellow citizens, neighbors, and colleagues.

Of course, many more introductions to Islam exist today than thirty years ago. I myself wrote *Islam: The Straight Path* and other books and articles that I have drawn upon in compiling this book. But such writings don't often reach the general reader. Many more people today have specific questions and are looking for direct answers, ones not easily found in historical and religious histories. *What Everyone Needs to Know About Islam* is meant to meet that need. Its primary purpose is to communicate what Muslims believe and why they do what they do. The book is not designed to be read from cover to cover; readers can look for answers to specific questions of interest to them. Because each question and answer is self-contained (it does not presume previous knowledge or that one has read previous answers), some material will appear in more than one answer.

Many of the questions, which have come from people in very diverse audiences, reflect a predisposition to believe that there is something profoundly wrong with Islam and Muslims. This underlying belief can result in the unconscious application of a double standard, approaching Islam differently than we would Judaism or Christianity when discussing how religion relates to extremism, militancy, violence, and terrorism. While we accept historical development in our own faiths with respect to pluralism, human rights, the status of women, and democratization, there is often a presumption that change is impossible in Islam.

I have had the good fortune to study, observe, and teach several religions, in particular Christianity and Islam as well as Judaism, Hinduism, and Buddhism. All these faiths have given meaning to and transformed the lives of millions throughout history. Regrettably, all also have had their dark side; religions that preach compassion, justice, and peace have been used—or abused—by extremists and militants. All are challenged in our modern and postmodern world to embrace a pluralism that balances affirmation of the truth of their faith with a respect for the truth to be found in others. For religion should be about righteousness, not self-righteousness.

The encounter between the West and the Muslim world, between Islam and the Judeo-Christian tradition, is not a clash of two separate and antithetical worlds. Jews, Christians, and Muslims are children of Abraham, part of a Judeo-Christian-Islamic tradition. The world of Islam is global; its capitals and centers are not only Cairo, Damascus, Mecca, Jerusalem, Istanbul, Islamabad, Kuala Lumpur, and Jakarta but also London, Paris, Marseilles, Bonn, New York, Detroit, and Washington. Our common future demands a new more inclusive sense of pluralism and tolerance built upon mutual understanding and respect. If we are ever to achieve such mutual understanding, an essential part of the package must be knowledge of what Islam teaches and what Muslims believe about Islam as well as what we believe about them.

# ACKNOWLEDGMENTS

In rendering translations of the Quran, I have consulted several very useful translations: Ahmed Ali: *Al-Qu'ran: A Contemporary Translation*, A. Yusuf Ali: *The Koran: Text, Translation and Commentary*, Muhammad Asad: *The Message of the Quran*, and Majid Fakhry: *The Qur'an: A Modern English Version*. I selected those that brought the greatest clarity. Where necessary I revised or provided my own translations.

I am especially indebted to Natana De Long-Bas, my senior research assistant. Her work on this project as on others was always quick and consistently excellent. Clare Merrill, Assistant Director, and Lesley Sebastian, Administrative Assistant of the Center for Muslim-Christian Understanding at Georgetown, kept things running as smoothly as possible, enabling me to work quickly and efficiently on the book as well as balance all my other obligations and activities.

I am grateful to several colleagues and friends who read all or portions of the manuscript, providing important feedback and suggestions: Hibba Abughideiri, Jonathan Brown, Khaled Abou El Fadl, Sherman Jackson, Alex Kronemer, and John Voll. Cynthia Read, my longtime editor at Oxford, carefully reviewed each chapter and provided invaluable feedback even when on vacation. Joellyn Ausanka oversaw the production process with the remarkable professionalism that I had come to so admire when working with her on *Unholy War: Terror in the Name of Islam*.

Jean Esposito, my wife, partner, and best friend, was there from conception to birth. The Q & A format was her idea, and only her enthusiasm, conviction, and collaboration made it happen. Like *Unholy War,* this book is in every sense of the words as much her book as mine. My parents, John and Mary Esposito, and my brothers, Lou and Rick, remain supportive in so many subtle ways. Finally, I wish to acknowledge all my Muslim friends and colleagues who over the years have given me their friendship and been a primary source for understanding Islam.

# WHAT EVERYONE
# NEEDS TO KNOW
# ABOUT ISLAM

# GENERAL INFORMATION

## Why do we need to know about Islam?

- Islam is the second largest religion in the world (after Christianity) and will soon be the second largest religion in America.

- Muslims are and will increasingly be our neighbors, colleagues at work, and fellow citizens.

- Although Islam is similar in many ways to Judaism and Christianity, most Americans and Europeans think of Muslims as strange, foreign, and frightening, inevitably linked to headline terrorist events. This state of affairs needs to change—and *can* change with better information and deeper understanding.

- We must put an end to the spiral of fear, hatred, and violence, spawned by ignorance, that no longer only afflicts other countries but has come home to America.

## Are all Muslims the same?

Since we are more familiar with Christianity, we know without thinking that there is great diversity in Christianity. Christianity expresses itself in many forms and contexts. There are different Christian churches or sects (from Baptists to Unitarians, Roman Catholics to Greek and Russian Orthodox), existing in different cultures (Middle Eastern, European, Asian, and African). The result is a diversity of beliefs and practices within what we call Christianity. So too, although Muslims maintain that there is one divinely revealed and mandated Islam, there are many Muslim interpretations of Islam. There are two major branches, Sunni (85 percent of the world's Muslims) and Shii (15 percent). Within them are diverse schools of theology and law. In addition, Islam has a rich mystical tradition that includes many Sufi orders or brotherhoods. Islam represents a basic unity of belief within a rich cultural diversity. Islamic practice expresses itself in different ways within a vast array of cultures that extend from North Africa to Southeast Asia as well as Europe and America. (See pages 39–58 for more specific questions on this topic.)

### *Where do most Muslims live?*

Muslims represent the majority population in fifty-six countries worldwide, including Indonesia, Bangladesh, Pakistan, Egypt, Iraq, and Nigeria. In addition, significant Muslim populations can be found in India, China, the Central Asian Republics, and Russia as well as Europe and America. Contrary to popular assumption, the majority of Muslims are not Arab. In fact only 20 percent of the world's 1.2 billion Muslims originate from Arab countries. The largest Muslim communities are to be found in Indonesia, Pakistan, Bangladesh, and India.

In recent decades, Islam has gone from being invisible in America and Europe to being a prominent feature in the religious landscape. Muslims represent a broad spectrum of racial and ethnic groups. Racial and ethnic diversity in Islam is represented by two broad Muslim groups: indigenous and immigrant. In American, in addition to indigenous African-American Muslims, prominent immigrant ethnic groups include Arabs, Pakistanis, Afghanis, Africans, Albanians, Bangladeshis, Bosnians, Indians, Iranians, Malaysians, Indonesians, and Turks.

# FAITH AND PRACTICE

## *What do Muslims believe?*

Like Jews and Christians, Muslims are monotheists. They believe in one God, the creator, sustainer, ruler, and judge of the universe. Muslims believe in prophets, not just the Prophet Muhammad but the prophets of the Hebrew Bible, including Abraham and Moses, and of the New Testament, Jesus and John the Baptist. They also believe in angels, heaven, hell, and the Day of Judgment. Islam acknowledges that God's revelation was received in the Torah, the Psalms, the Gospels, and the Quran: "We sent Jesus the son of Mary, confirming the Torah that had come before him: We sent him the Gospel in which is guidance and light, and confirmation of the Torah that had come before him, a guidance and an admonition to those who fear God" (Quran 5:46). Thus Muslims view Jews and Christians as "People of the Book," a community of believers who received revelations, through prophets, in the form of scriptures or revealed books from God.

As Christians view their revelation as both fulfilling and completing the revelation of the Old Testament, Muslims believe that the Prophet Muhammad received his revelations from God through the angel Gabriel to correct human error that had made its way into the scriptures and belief systems of Judaism and Christianity. Therefore, Muslims believe that Islam is not a new religion with a new scripture. Far from being the youngest of the major monotheistic world religions, from a Muslim point of view Islam is the oldest because it represents the original as well as the final revelation of the God of Abraham, Moses, Jesus, and Muhammad: "He established for you the same religion as that which He established for Noah, that which We have sent to you as inspiration through Abraham, Moses, and Jesus, namely that you should remain steadfast in religion and make no divisions within it" (Quran 42:13).

### Why do Muslims say they are descended from Abraham?

Muslims see themselves, along with Jews and Christians, as children of Abraham, belonging to different branches of the same religious family. The Quran and the Old Testament both tell the story of Abraham, Sarah, and Hagar, Sarah's Egyptian servant. While Jews and Christians are descended from Abraham and his wife Sarah through their son Isaac, Muslims trace their religious roots back to Abraham through Ismail, his firstborn son by Hagar.

According to both Hebrew and Muslim scripture, when after many years Sarah did not conceive a child, she urged Abraham to sleep with her maidservant, Hagar, so that he might have an heir. The child who was the result of that union was a boy named Ismail. After Ismail's birth, Sarah too finally became pregnant and gave birth to Isaac. She then became jealous of Ismail, who as firstborn would be the prime inheritor and overshadow her own son Isaac. So she pressured Abraham to send Hagar and Ismail away. Abraham reluctantly let Hagar and his son go, because God promised that He would make Ismail the father of a great nation. Islamic sources say that Hagar and Ismail ended up in the vicinity of Mecca in Arabia, and both scriptures say that they nearly died but were saved by a spring that miraculously gushed from the desert.

Islamic scripture and tradition tell a rich story about how father and son were reunited. This reunion gave rise to two of the most visible symbols of Islam. According to Islamic sources, Abraham learned that Hagar and Ismail were alive and found them living near present-day Mecca. After hearing of Hagar's harrowing experiences in the desert and the story of the miracle that saved them, he and Ismail rebuilt the Kaaba, believed to have been originally built by Adam, as a temple to the one true God. It is for this reason that Muslims across the globe turn in the direction of the Kaaba when they pray, as a unifying act of worship of the one true God. Today the Kaaba is considered the most sacred place in the Muslim world. Its distinctive cube shape with its black covering is one of the most familiar symbols in Islam. (See page 23, "What is the Kaaba?") Muslim scripture also tells that Abraham established the rites of the sacred pilgrimage to Mecca, many of which recreate Hagar's experiences there. The pilgrimage attracts over two million people annually and is another striking symbol of the faith. (See page 22, "What do Muslims do on the pilgrimage to Mecca?")

There is one significant difference in the biblical and Islamic accounts of the Abraham story. Contrary to the biblical tradition (Genesis 22:1–2), most Islamic scholars designate Ismail rather than Isaac as the intended victim in the story of Abraham's willingness to sacrifice his son at God's command (Quran 37:99–113).

## How did Islam originate?

Like Judaism and Christianity, Islam originated in the Middle East. It was not a totally new monotheistic religion that sprang up in isolation. Belief in one God, monotheism, had been flourishing for many centuries. Knowledge of Judaism, Christianity, and Zoroastrianism had been brought to Mecca in Arabia by foreign caravan trade as well as through the travels and contacts of Meccan traders throughout the Middle East. Moreover, Christian, Zoroastrian, and Jewish tribes lived in Arabia.

In the sixth century, Mecca was emerging as a new commercial center with vast new wealth but also with a growing division between rich and poor, challenging the traditional system of Arab tribal values and social security. This was the time and social environment in which the Prophet Muhammad preached the message of the Quran, which formed the basis for the religion we know as Islam, calling all to return to the worship of the one true God and a socially just society.

Muslims believe that God sent revelations first to Moses (as found in the Hebrew scriptures, the Torah), then to Jesus (the Gospel), and finally to Muhammad (through the Islamic scripture, the Quran). Muhammad is not considered the founder of the new religion of Islam. Like the biblical prophets who came before him, he was a religious reformer. Muhammad said that he did not bring a new message from a new God but called people back to the one true God and to a way of life they had forgotten or deviated from.

Because it is not a new revelation, the Quran contains many references to stories and figures in the Old and New Testaments, including Adam and Eve, Abraham and Moses, David and Solomon, and Jesus and Mary. Islam and worship of Allah—the Arabic word for God, meaning literally "the God"—was a return in the midst of a polytheistic society to the forgotten past, to the faith of the first monotheist, Abraham.

To Muhammad, most of his contemporaries in Mecca, with its tribal polytheism, lived in ignorance of the one true God and His will as revealed to the prophets Adam, Abraham, Moses, and Jesus. The revelations Muhammad received led him to believe that Jews and Christians over time had distorted God's original message to Moses and later to Jesus. Thus the Torah and the Gospels were seen by Muslims as a combination of original revelation and later human additions such as the elevation of Jesus from a prophet to the son of God.

The revelations Muhammad received were calls to religious and social reform. They emphasized social justice (concern for the rights of women, widows, and orphans), corrected distortions to God's revelations in Judaism and Christianity, and warned that many had strayed from the message of God and his prophets. They called upon all to return to what the Quran refers to as the straight path of Islam or the path of God, revealed one final time to Muhammad, the last or "seal" of the prophets.

## What is the Muslim scripture?

*Quran* (sometimes written *Koran*) means "recitation" in Arabic. The Quran is the Muslim scripture. It contains the revelations received by the Prophet Muhammad from God through the angel Gabriel. Muhammad, who was illiterate, functioned as God's intermediary; he was told to "recite" the revelation he received. For Muslims, Muhammad was neither the author nor editor of the Quran. Therefore, the Quran is the eternal, literal word of God, preserved in the Arabic language in which it was revealed and placed in an order that was commanded by divine revelation. Over a period of twenty-three years, from Muhammad's fortieth year until his death in 632, the Quran's 114 chapters (called *surahs*) were revealed to him.

Muslims believe that the Quran was initially preserved in oral and written form during the lifetime of the Prophet. The entire text was finally collected in an official standardized version some fifteen or twenty years after his death. The Quran is approximately four-fifths the size of the New Testament. Its chapters were assembled from the longest chapter to the shortest, not edited or organized thematically. This format has proved frustrating to many non-Muslims, who find the text disjointed or disorganized from their point of view. However, it enables a believer to simply open the text at random and start reciting at the beginning of any paragraph, since each represents a lesson to be learned and reflected upon.

Recitation of the Quran is central to a Muslim's life; many Muslims memorize the Quran in its entirety. Recitation reinforces what Muslims see as the miracle of hearing the actual word of God expressed by the human voice. There are many examples throughout history of those who were drawn to and converted to Islam upon hearing the Quran recited. Muslims recite passages from the Quran that are included in their five daily prayers; musical and poetic recitations of Quranic verses serve as an introduction to every community event, from weddings and funerals to lectures and business dinners. Quran recitations are performed before stadiums of devout and enthusiastic Muslims whose numbers resemble those of Americans or Europeans attending an opera or concert. Many Muslims experience deep aesthetic pleasure from listening to the rich, resonant, rhyming prose, with its repetitions and subtle inflections.

## *Why is Arabic so important in Islam?*

Muslims believe that the Quran, as well as the Torah and the Gospels, is based on a tablet written in Arabic that exists in heaven with God. They believe that the teachings of these scriptures, revealed at different times in history, originate from this source. The Quran, recited by Muhammad as it was revealed to him by the angels, and later recorded in Arabic, is thus believed to be the direct word of God. All Muslims, regardless of their native language, memorize and recite the Quran in Arabic, the language in which it was revealed, whether they fully understand this language or not. So too, all over the world, regardless of their local language, when Muslims pray they do so in Arabic. Until modern times, the Quran was printed in Arabic only. Even now, in translations, which more correctly are viewed by Muslims as "interpretations," the Arabic text is often printed alongside.

The oral recitation of the Quran has remained a powerful source of inspiration to the present day. Chanting of the Quran in Arabic is an art form, and Quran reciters are held in an esteem comparable to that of opera stars in the West. Recordings of the Quran are enjoyed for their aesthetic as well as their religious value. Walking in the streets of a Muslim country, a visitor is bound to hear the Quran being recited on radios or cassettes in shops or passing taxis. Crowds fill stadiums throughout the Islamic world for public Quran recitation contests. Memorization of the entire Quran brings great prestige as well as merit.

### What role does Muhammad play in Muslim life?

During his lifetime and throughout the following centuries, the Prophet Muhammad has been the ideal model for Muslims to follow as they strive to do God's will. Islam places great emphasis upon action—exhorting Muslims to strive, to make an effort, to do their best. Some Muslims say that Muhammad is the "living Quran," the witness whose words and behavior reveal God's will. In contrast to the often spiritualized Christian view of Jesus, Muslims look upon Muhammad as both a prophet and a very human figure, one who had great political as well as spiritual insights. Thus Muslims look to Muhammad's example for guidance in all aspects of life: how to treat friends as well as enemies, what to eat and drink, how to mourn and celebrate. The importance given to Muhammad's example is a variation on a tradition that originated with pre-Islamic Arabian tribes who preserved their ideals and norms in what was called their *sunnah* (trodden path). These were the tribal customs, the traditions handed down from previous generations by word and example. Muhammad reformed these practices, and as a result his Sunnah (his words and deeds) became the norm for Muslim community life.

Muhammad's life translated the guidance revealed in the Quran into action; he lived the revelation, giving concrete form to the laws that God revealed for the various conditions of ordinary human life. For Islam, no aspect of life is outside the realm of religion. Muslims' observations or remembrances of what the Prophet said and did were passed on orally and in writing through "traditions" (*hadith*). The hadith deal with all aspects of Muhammad's life, intensely personal as well as public, social, and political. Thus, when Muslims pray or make the pilgrimage to Mecca, they try to pray as the Prophet prayed, without adding to or subtracting from the way Muhammad is said to have worshipped. This is not to imply that Muslims worship Muhammad in any way. Rather, traditions of the Prophet provide guidance regarding personal hygiene, dress, eating, treatment of spouses, diplomacy, and warfare. The detailed records of Muhammad's actions in war and peace, his interactions with family, friends, and foes, his judgments in good and bad times, and his decisions when under siege and when victorious recall and reinforce for Muslims what it takes to follow the word of God.

## Was Muhammad a prophet like the prophets in the Bible?

In Islam the concept of prophecy is broader than in Judaism and Christianity. Muslims distinguish between "prophets" and "messengers," to whom God gives a message for a community in book form. Unlike prophets, God's messengers are assured success by God. While all messengers are prophets, not all prophets are messengers. The word *prophet* is applied to Abraham, Noah, Joseph, and John the Baptist as well as nonbiblical prophets of Arabia like Hud and Salih. *Messenger* is limited to the prophets Moses, Jesus, and Muhammad, whose revelations were preserved in scriptural form.

## Why is so much known about Muhammad's life?

Muslims believe that Muhammad not only received God's final revelation to humankind but also perfectly lived out the revelation he received. Thus he is sometimes referred to as the "living Quran." Muhammad was and is the model of the Muslim ideal to be emulated by all believers. While Muhammad was alive, people could go directly to him to request his advice or opinion about any topic. When Muhammad died, the Muslim community lost its direct channel of revelation.

Because Muslims believe that Muhammad's words and actions serve as a living example of the meaning of the Quran, the early Muslim community was anxious to preserve as many memories of his words and actions as possible. Narrative stories about the Prophet's example (Sunnah), known as the *hadith* (traditions) of the Prophet, record many aspects of Muhammad's life, including religious belief and ritual, eating, dress, personal hygiene, marriage, treatment of spouses, diplomacy, and warfare. These detailed records of Muhammad's actions in war and peace, his interactions with family, friends, and foes, his judgments in good and bad times, and his decisions when under siege and when victorious recall and reinforce for Muslims what it takes to follow the word of God. Excluded from imitation is anything that belonged to his specific capacity as Prophet.

The hadith were collected over a period of several hundred years. In many cases, there are several hadith that deal with the same situation, since many people were typically present when Muhammad was answering questions from the Muslim community. Although there are many hadith collections, two in particular, those compiled by Muslim ibn al-Hajjaj and Ismail al-Bukhari, enjoy special authoritative status in Sunni Islam.

Early on, given the proliferation of traditions of the Prophet, questions quickly arose about the authenticity of the hadith; as a result, a special science of hadith criticism was developed in order to authenticate them. The most important method of hadith authentication was through verification of the chain of transmitters. Most began with the format that so-and-so told so-and-so that she or he heard from so-and-so, tracing the line of transmitters back to either Muhammad himself or one of his Companions who had reported that Muhammad said or did something. Great care was taken to determine the honesty of the various transmitters and whether they could possibly have known the person from whom they received the hadith. If the chain of transmitters could be proven possible, then the hadith was accepted as authentic.

A second method of hadith criticism focused on the content of the hadith rather than just the chain of transmitters. Those who examined the content attempted to verify that the hadith was consistent with both the Quran and other hadith on a similar topic. In cases where two hadith conflict, religious scholars use the Quran as the final authority with respect to content, regardless of who the transmitter was.

Although some modern scholars, both non-Muslim and Muslims, have raised questions about the authenticity of the hadith, the majority of Muslims continue to consider the hadith as scripture and cite them as evidence of God's commands about a particular topic. Equally important, whether or not they came directly from Muhammad, the traditions of the Prophet provide a rich religious and social history, a substantial record of how the Prophet of Islam has been and continues to be regarded by the Muslim community, and insight into the issues and debates within early Islamic history.

## Did Muhammad have multiple wives?

During the prime of his life, Muhammad had one wife, Khadija, for twenty-four years, until her death when he was forty-nine. Much is recorded about Muhammad's relationship with Khadija, who served as his closest confidante and comforter and strongest supporter. They had six children, two sons who died in infancy and four daughters.

After her death Muhammad started to contract other marriages, all but one of them to widows. As was customary for Arab chiefs, some of these marriages were contracted to cement political alliances. Others were marriages to wives of his companions who had fallen in combat, women who were in need of protection. Remarriage for widows was difficult in a society that placed a high value on a bride's virginity. However, talk of the political and social motives behind many of Muhammad's marriages should not obscure the fact that Muhammad was attracted to and enjoyed the company of women as friends as well as spouses. His life reflects the Islamic outlook on marriage and sexuality, found in both revelation and Prophetic traditions, which emphasizes the importance of family and views sex as a gift from God to be enjoyed within the bonds of marriage.

## What do Muslims believe about a worldwide Muslim community (ummah)?

Muslims believe that they are members of a worldwide Muslim community, known as the *ummah*, united by a religious bond that transcends tribal, ethnic, and national identities. This belief is based upon Quran 2:143, which declares that God created the Muslim ummah to serve as witnesses of God's guidance to the nations.

Islam was revealed in a time and place in which tribal loyalty was considered a person's most important identification. The individual's status was based upon membership in a particular tribe. Islam declared the absolute equality of all believers. The primary identity of the Muslim was as a Muslim, rather than as a member of a tribe, ethnicity, or gender. This notion of radical egalitarianism shattered the importance of tribal identities and fostered the belief that Muslims should always defend and protect other Muslims. Quran 9:71 says: "The believers, men and women, are protectors of one another. They enjoin what is just and forbid what is evil. They

observe regular prayers, regularly give alms, and obey God
and His Messenger [i.e., Muhammad]. On them will God pour
His mercy, for God is exalted in power, wise."

*Ummah* is often used to refer to the essential unity of all
Muslims, despite their diverse geographical and cultural set-
tings. The traditions of the Prophet *(hadith)* speak of the ummah
as the spiritual, nonterritorial community of Muslims that is
distinguished and united by the shared beliefs of its members.
This concept became particularly important during the nine-
teenth-century era of European colonialism and the rise of
nationalism. Islamic resistance movements called for the defense of the ummah against European intrusions throughout
the Islamic world. The Ottoman Empire also appealed to the
unity of the ummah as a way of reinvigorating Islamic solidarity. Nationalists, although trying to unite their countries on
the basis of national loyalty, did not challenge the authority of
the concept of the ummah and in fact used it as the basis for
calling for political unity. Although nationalists since the 1960s
have called for a separation of national and religious identities, Islamists continue to support the notion of membership
in the ummah as the primary identity for all Muslims, rather
than ethnic, linguistic, or geographic identities. Contemporary Muslims still believe in the ummah as a social identity,
despite the secularization of public life and contemporary emphasis on national political identities.

Muslims have been commanded to protect each other and
to consider their identities as Muslims to be more important
than any other identities they might have. They refer to their
membership in the Muslim ummah as the reason for their concern for Muslims throughout the world. Causes that have received broad attention from the worldwide Muslim community
include the Afghan struggle against Soviet occupation from

1979 to 1989, ethnic cleansing of Bosnian Muslims in 1994 and of Kosovar Albanian Muslims in 1997, and the ongoing plight of the Palestinians. Muslims have also been active in fund-raising to assist victims of natural disasters in the Muslim world, such as earthquakes in Turkey and Afghanistan.

## *What are the core beliefs that unite all Muslims?*

Despite a rich diversity in Islamic practice, there are five simple required observances prescribed in the Quran that all practicing Muslims accept and follow. These *"Pillars of Islam"* represent the core and common denominator that unites all Muslims and distinguishes Islam from other religions. Following the Pillars of Islam requires dedication of your mind, feelings, body, time, energies, and possessions. Meeting the obligations required by the Pillars reinforces an ongoing presence of God in Muslims' lives and reminds them of their membership in a single worldwide community of believers.

1. The first Pillar is called the *Declaration of Faith*. A Muslim is one who bears witness, who testifies that "there is no god but God [Allah] and Muhammad is the messenger of God." This declaration is known as the *shahada* (witness, testimony). Allah is the Arabic name for God, just as Yahweh is the Hebrew name for God used in the Old Testament. To become a Muslim, one need only make this simple proclamation.

The first part of this proclamation affirms Islam's absolute monotheism, the uncompromising belief in the oneness or unity of God, as well as the doctrine that association of anything else with God is idolatry and the one unforgivable sin. As we see in Quran 4:48: "God does not forgive anyone for associating something with Him, while He does forgive whomever He wishes to for anything else. Anyone who gives God associates [partners] has invented an awful sin." This helps us to understand the Islamic belief that its revelation is intended to correct such departures from the "straight path" as the Christian concept of the Trinity and veneration of the Virgin Mary in Catholicism.

The second part of the confession of faith asserts that Muhammad is not only a prophet but also a messenger of God, a higher role also played by Moses and Jesus before him. For Muslims, Muhammad is the vehicle for the last and final revelation. In accepting Muhammad as the "seal of the prophets," they believe that his prophecy confirms and completes all of the revealed messages, beginning with Adam's. In addition, somewhat like Jesus Christ, Muhammad serves as the preeminent role model through his life example. The believer's effort to follow Muhammad's example reflects the emphasis of Islam on practice and action. In this regard Islam is more like Judaism, with its emphasis upon the law, than Christianity, which gives greater importance to doctrines or dogma. This practical orientation of Islam is reflected in the remaining four Pillars of Islam.

2. The second Pillar of Islam is *Prayer* (*salat*). Muslims pray (or, perhaps more correctly, worship) five times throughout the day: at daybreak, noon, midafternoon, sunset, and evening. Although the times for prayer and the ritual actions were not specified in the Quran, Muhammad established them.

In many Muslim countries, reminders to pray, or "calls to prayer," echo out across the rooftops. Aided by a megaphone, from high atop a mosque's minaret, the muezzin calls out:

> God is most great [Allahu Akbar], God is most great, God is most great, God is most great, I witness that there is no god but God [Allah]; I witness that there is no god but God. I

witness that Muhammad is the messenger of God. I witness that Muhammad is the messenger of God. Come to prayer; come to prayer! Come to prosperity; come to prosperity! God is most great. God is most great. There is no god but God.

These reminders throughout the day help to keep believers mindful of God in the midst of everyday concerns about work and family with all their attractions and distractions. It strengthens the conscience, reaffirms total dependence on God, and puts worldly concerns within the perspective of death, the last judgment, and the afterlife.

The prayers consist of recitations from the Quran in Arabic and glorification of God. These are accompanied by a sequence of movements: standing, bowing, kneeling, touching the ground with one's forehead, and sitting. Both the recitations and accompanying movements express submission, humility, and adoration of God. Muslims can pray in any clean environment, alone or together, in a mosque or at home, at work or on the road, indoors or out. It is considered preferable and more meritorious to pray with others, if possible, as one body united in the worship of God, demonstrating discipline, brotherhood, equality, and solidarity.

As they prepare to pray, Muslims face Mecca, the holy city that houses the Kaaba (the house of God believed to have been built by Abraham and his son Ismail). Each act of worship begins with the declaration that "God is most great" ("Allahu Akbar") and is followed by fixed prayers that include the opening verse of the Quran.

At the end of the prayer, the *shahada* (declaration of faith) is again recited, and the "peace greeting"—"Peace be upon all of you and the mercy and blessings of God"—is repeated twice.

3. The third Pillar of Islam is called the *Zakat*, which means "purification." Like prayer, which is both an individual and communal responsibility, zakat expresses a Muslim's worship of and thanksgiving to God by supporting the poor. It requires an annual contribution of 2.5 percent of an individual's wealth and assets, not merely a percentage of annual income. In Islam, the true owner of things is not man but God. People are given their wealth as a trust from God. Therefore, zakat is not viewed as "charity"; it is an obligation for those who have received their wealth from God to respond to the needs of less fortunate members of the community. The Quran (9:60) as well as Islamic law stipulates that alms are to be used to support the poor, orphans, and widows, to free slaves and debtors, and to support those working in the "cause of God" (e.g., construction of mosques, religious schools, and hospitals). Zakat, developed fourteen hundred years ago, functions as a form of social security in a Muslim society. In Shii Islam, in addition to the zakat, which is not limited to 2.5 percent, believers pay a religious tax (*khums*) on their income to a religious leader. This is used to support the poor and needy.

4. The fourth Pillar of Islam, the *Fast of Ramadan*, occurs once each year during the month of Ramadan, the ninth month of the Islamic calendar and the month in which the first revelation of the Quran came to Muhammad. During this month-long fast, Muslims whose health permits must abstain from dawn to sunset from food, drink, and sexual activity. Fasting is a practice common to many religions, sometimes undertaken as penance, sometimes to free us from undue focus on physical needs and appetites. In Islam the discipline of the Ramadan fast is intended to stimulate reflection on human frailty and dependence upon God, focus on spiritual goals and values, and identification with and response to the less fortunate.

At dusk the fast is broken with a light meal popularly referred to as breakfast. Families and friends share a special late evening meal together, often including special foods and sweets served only at this time of the year. Many go to the mosque for the evening prayer, followed by special prayers recited only during Ramadan. Some will recite the entire Quran (one-thirtieth each night of the month) as a special act of piety, and public recitations of the Quran or Sufi chanting can be heard throughout the evening. Families rise before sunrise to take their first meal of the day, which must sustain them until sunset.

Near the end of Ramadan (the twenty-seventh day) Muslims commemorate the "Night of Power" when Muhammad first received God's revelation. The month of Ramadan ends with one of the two major Islamic celebrations, the Feast of the Breaking of the Fast, called Eid al-Fitr, which resembles Christmas in its spirit of joyfulness, special celebrations, and gift giving.

5. The fifth Pillar is the *Pilgrimage or Hajj* to Mecca in Saudi Arabia. At least once in his or her lifetime, every adult Muslim who is physically and financially able is required to make the sacrifice of time, possessions, status, and normal comforts necessary to make this pilgrimage, becoming a pilgrim totally at God's service. The pilgrimage season follows Ramadan. Every year over two million believers representing a tremendous diversity of cultures and languages travel from all over the world to the holy city of Mecca to form one community living their faith. In addition to the hajj there is a devotional ritual that is referred to as the "lesser pilgrimage." It is called the *umrah* (visitation) and involves visiting the holy sites at other times of the year. Many who are on pilgrimage also perform the umrah rituals before, during, or after the hajj. However, performing the umrah does not fulfill the hajj obligation.

## What do Muslims do on the pilgrimage to Mecca?

Those who participate in the pilgrimage wear simple garments, two seamless white cloths for men and an outfit that entirely covers the body, except face and hands, for women. These coverings symbolize purity as well as the unity and equality of all believers.

As the pilgrims approach Mecca they shout "I am here, O Lord, I am here!" When they enter Mecca their first obligation is to go to the Kaaba, which is located inside the compound of the Grand Mosque. (See page 23, "What is the Kaaba?") The crowds of pilgrims move counterclockwise around the Kaaba seven times. This circumambulation, like prayer, symbolizes the believer's entry into the divine presence.

In the days that follow, pilgrims participate in a variety of ritual actions and ceremonies symbolizing key religious events. They walk and sometimes run along a quarter-mile corridor of the Grand Mosque seven times to commemorate Hagar's frantic search in the desert for water for her son Ismail. This rite, in great contrast to the circumambulation of the Kaaba, which centers on spiritual contact with God, symbolizes humankind's ongoing effort, movement, and struggle through life, expressing a believer's persistence in life's struggle for survival. The pilgrims drink water from the well, called Zamzam (meaning "bubbling"), which is located within the Grand Mosque, where Muslims believe God provided water for Hagar and Ismail. They assemble for a day at Arafat, a vast, empty plain, in commemoration of the final pilgrimage of Muhammad, who delivered his farewell sermon to his people from the Mount of Mercy, a hill in the middle of the plain. They symbolically reject the devil, the source of all evil, by throwing stones at three pillars that stand at the site where Satan met Abraham and Ismail and tempted them to disobey God when Abraham was preparing to sacrifice his son in obedience to God's command.

## *What is the Kaaba?*

The Kaaba is seen as the most sacred space in the Muslim world, the site to which hundreds of millions of Muslims throughout the world turn each day when they pray.

Located inside the compound of the Grand Mosque at Mecca, the Kaaba (literally, "cube") is a cube-shaped structure known as the "House of God." It contains the sacred Black Stone, a meteorite believed to have been placed by Abraham and Ismail in a corner of the Kaaba, a symbol of God's covenant with Abraham and Ismail and by extension with the Muslim community itself. The Kaaba is approximately forty-five feet high and thirty-three by fifty feet wide and is draped with a woven black cloth embellished with Quranic verses embroidered in gold.

The Kaaba is considered the first house of worship of the one God, originally built by Adam and replicating the heavenly House of God, which contains the divine throne that is circumambulated by the angels. This heavenly ritual is reenacted during the *hajj* (pilgrimage to Mecca) by pilgrims who circumambulate the Kaaba seven times, symbolizing their entry before the divine presence. Adam's Kaaba is believed to have been destroyed by the neglect of believers and the flood, but according to the Quran (2:127) Abraham and his son Ismail rebuilt the holy house. However, by the time of Muhammad the Kaaba was under the control of the Quraysh of Mecca, who used it as a shrine for the tribal gods and idols of Arabia.

The Quraysh held an annual pilgrimage to the Kaaba and a fair that attracted pilgrims from all over Arabia.

Tradition tells us that one of the first things Muhammad did when he returned from exile and triumphantly entered Mecca was to cleanse the Kaaba of its 360 idols and restore the "religion of Abraham," the worship of the one true God.

## *What is the significance of Mecca?*

Mecca, in Saudi Arabia, is the birthplace of the Prophet Muhammad and the most sacred location in the Islamic world. It is the site of the Grand Mosque, which houses the Kaaba. (See page 23, "What is the Kaaba?") Millions of Muslims travel there each year from all over the world to perform the *hajj*. Mecca is seen as housing the spiritual center of the earth, where actions of worship such as the circumambulation of the Kaaba (see page 22, "What do Muslims do on the pilgrimage to Mecca?") are believed to be duplicated in heaven at the Throne of God. Mecca, like Medina, is closed to non-Muslims.

## *How do Muslims pray?*

Prayer, one of the Five Pillars of Islam, is central in the life of a Muslim. Here are some highlights:

Five times each day, hundreds of millions of Muslims face Mecca (holiest city of Islam, birthplace of Muhammad, and site of the Kaaba, or House of God) to pray—at daybreak, noontime, midafternoon, sunset, and evening. These five obligatory prayers have to be performed in Arabic, regardless of the native tongue of the worshipper. Each part of the prayer has its function within this daily ritual and is designed to combine meditation, devotion, moral elevation, and physical exercise. Prayers can be performed individually or in congregation.

The actions and words a Muslim uses during the prayer demonstrate his or her ultimate submission to God. This process combines faith and practice, putting into action what is expressed in the First Pillar of Islam, in which Muslims proclaim their belief in the one God and in Muhammad as God's messenger.

Preparing to meet and address the Lord, Muslims perform a ritual ablution, or cleansing, to ensure that they are in a state of spiritual and physical purity. First, they cleanse their minds and hearts from worldly thoughts and concerns, concentrating on God and the blessings he has given them. Second, they wash hands and face, arms up to the elbow, and feet, then say, "I bear witness that there is no god but God; He has no partner; and I bear witness that Muhammad is His servant and messenger." This purification process is as spiritual as it is physical, as can be seen in the fact that sand can be used if water is not available. The objective is for the mind and body to be clean as Muslims approach or put themselves in the presence of God.

The movements Muslims perform while praying, individually or in groups, reflect past customs used when entering the presence of great kings or rulers: raising our hands in greeting, bowing, and finally prostrating ourselves before this great power. Worshippers begin by raising their hands and proclaiming God's greatness ("Allahu Akbar"—God is most great). Then, folding their hands over stomach or chest or leaving them at their sides, they stand upright and recite what has been described as the essential message of the Quran, the opening discourse:

Praise be to God, Lord of the Worlds; the Beneficent, the Merciful; Master of the Day of Judgment. You alone do we worship and from you alone do we seek aid. Show us the Straight Way, the way of those upon whom You have bestowed Your grace, not of those who have earned Your wrath or who go astray. (Quran 1:2–6)

After reciting another (this time self-selected) verse from the Quran, Muslims bow and proclaim, "Glory to God in the Highest," three times. Returning to an upright position, they say, "God hears the one who praises Him" and "Our Lord, all praise belongs to you!"

The next phase of worship involves what is commonly called "prostration" in English, although it does not involve lying down at full length. The position Muslims take represents an expression of ultimate submission. Before beginning the act of prostration, Muslims first repeat, "Allahu Akbar" (God is most great). Then they fall to their knees, placing hands flat on the ground and bringing their foreheads down between their hands to touch the ground. While in this bowing position, Muslims recite three times, "Glory to the Lord Most High!" After this, they stand up and repeat the entire cycle of prayer.

Prayer includes sitting on the heels and reciting a formula known as "the witnessing" because it contains the declaration of Muslim faith. The witnessing is followed by asking God's blessings for the first and last of God's Prophets, Abraham and Muhammad.

Finally, prayer is ended with an invocation of peace (*salam*). Worshippers turn their heads right and left and say, "May the peace, mercy, and blessings of Allah be upon you." Although this invocation is addressed to fellow believers on the right and left, some Muslims also believe they are addressing their guardian angels, who remain over their shoulders as they pray. After completing the obligatory prayers, Muslims can privately petition (*dua*) God regarding their individual needs. There are recommended prayer texts in Arabic for such individual needs and problems, but in these prayers the worshipper can also address God in his or her own native language and own words.

When Islam first appeared in the Middle East, it was common practice in the Byzantine and Sasanian empires to prostrate oneself before the Byzantine emperor (a Christian) and the Shah of Persia (a Zoroastrian), since both rulers were both king and high priest. However, Muslims historically were especially strong in refusing to prostrate themselves before anyone or anything but Allah. In the mid-seventh century the Tang Dynasty of China recorded that a delegation of Arab and Persian visitors refused to prostrate themselves in front of the emperor, who was believed to be the "Son of Heaven."

In modern times we can still find examples of prostration in other religions. To the present day Anglican and Catholic clergy prostrate themselves before the altar at the beginning of the Good Friday liturgy, and so do the ordinands in the rite of ordination. Members of some Catholic monastic orders regularly prostrate themselves instead of genuflecting before the blessed sacrament at the altar of Christ.

## *Do Muslims believe in angels?*

Like Jews and Christians, Muslims believe that angels are a part of God's creation. Angels act as God's agents and serve Him by protecting humans, relaying His messages, or performing a variety of other functions. For example, the angel Gabriel brought divine revelation to Muhammad; the angel Michael provides sustenance for human bodies and knowledge to human minds; the angel Israfil will sound the trumpet at the Final Judgment.

According to Islamic tradition, angels are created from light. Unlike humans, they do not have free will. They are absolutely obedient to God's commands and are everlastingly engaged in worship and service to Him. Many Muslims believe that two angels attend each human being, recording all of his or her words and actions up until the moment of death. They will present this account on the Day of Judgment.

## Do Muslims believe in heaven and hell?

Muslims do believe in heaven and hell, in eternal reward or punishment depending on whether human beings follow the will of God and act with justice and mercy toward others during their lifetime. The Quran frequently emphasizes the ultimate moral responsibility and accountability of each believer. On the Day of Judgment, a great cataclysmic cosmic event that will occur at a moment known only to God, all will be raised from the dead. God will judge each person by the standards brought by the person's community's prophets and scripture, using the record of each person's actions throughout his or her life that are recorded in the Book of Deeds: "Then those whose balance of good deeds is heavy will attain salvation, but those whose balance is light will have lost their souls and abide in Hell forever" (Quran 23:102–103)

The Quran's vision of the afterlife is both spiritual and physical. Bodies and souls will be joined, and the pleasures of heavenly gardens of bliss and the pain of hellfire will be fully experienced. The Garden of Paradise is a heavenly mansion of peace and bliss with flowing rivers, beautiful gardens, and cool drink from a shining stream. Quranic descriptions of heavenly bliss are life-affirming, emphasizing the beauty of creation and enjoyment of its pleasures within the limits set by God:

> Those who believe and do righteous deeds, they are the
> best of creatures. Their reward is with their Lord: Gardens
> of Paradise beneath which rivers flow. They will dwell
> therein forever, God well-pleased with them and they with
> Him. This is for those who hold their Lord in awe. (98:7–8)

Later traditions elaborated on the joys of paradise and the role of *houris,* or beautiful companions. The Quran makes no reference to a sexual role for the houris, but some Western critics have rendered *houris* as meaning "virgins" and seized upon one popular belief that has been used to motivate some Muslim suicide bombers. However, many Quranic commentators and most Muslims understand houris as virgins only in the sense of pure or purified souls.

Hell is a place of endless pain, suffering, torment, and despair, with roaring flames, fierce boiling waters, and scorching wind. The destiny of the damned, their eternal punishment, is a just punishment, the result of human choice:

> Verily, the sinners will be in the punishment of Hell, to re-
> main therein. It will not be lightened for them and they will
> be overwhelmed in despair. And we shall not be unjust to
> them, but it is they who have been unjust to themselves.
> (43:74–76)

The Quran's comprehensive and integrated view of life contrasts with Christianity's tendency to compartmentalize life into the sacred and profane, body and soul, sensual and spiritual. In contrast to the "spiritual" images of a more sedate, celibate, and blissful Paradise predominant in Christian visions of heaven, the Quran does not draw a distinction between enjoying the joys of beatific vision and those of the fruits of creation.

In modern times, more conservative and fundamentalist writers and religious leaders continue to appeal to literalist interpretations of the afterlife. Most contemporary Muslim commentary tends to emphasize the importance of moral responsibility and accountability in this life and its direct connection to divine justice with eternal reward and punishment without getting into explicit, concrete descriptions of the afterlife.

### Do Muslims believe in saints?

*Saint* in Arabic is somewhat equivalent to the Arabic word *wali*, which means "friend, helper, or patron." There is no mention of saints in the Quran, which emphasizes that God alone is the wali of believers and there is no helper but Him. In fact, the Quran warns about "intercession," seeking help from anyone but God. Therefore, some Muslims are opposed to the concept of sainthood as un-Islamic. They say that such beliefs and practices violate monotheism by potentially treating saints as if they are equal to God. Others, however, believe that there can be intercession with God's permission and that some receive a special favor from God allowing them to intercede for others. Certain saints are known for providing intercessions for particular causes: helping women to bear children, solving domestic problems, curing illnesses, or avoiding certain disasters.

The Christian and Islamic concepts of sainthood differ in a number of ways. Sainthood in Islam is not determined by Catholicism's method of canonization but rather by a more informal process of acclamation. The majority of popular saints are Sufi saints. (Sufis are the mystics of Islam; see page 56, "Are Sufis Muslims?") The tombs of Sufi saints are often the object of pilgrimage and a focal point for festivals and processions celebrating a saint's birth or death. Other Sufi saints are more remembered for their wise sayings, virtues, and miracles. A significant number of popular, Sufi, and legendary saints are women.

## *What do Muslims believe about Mary and Jesus?*

Mary, the mother of Jesus, is a prominent figure in Islam and the only woman mentioned by name in the Quran. The Quran upholds Mary as one of the four perfect examples of womanhood (66:12). An entire chapter, Surah 19, is dedicated to her and her history. Mary is mentioned more times in the Quran than in the entire New Testament, and more biographical information about her is contained in the Quran than in the New Testament.

The Quranic account of Mary includes the pregnancy of her mother, Anna, Mary's birth, the annunciations of the coming births of John the Baptist and Jesus, and affirmation of the virgin conception and birth of Jesus: "[Remember] her who preserved her chastity, into whom We breathed a life from Us, and made her and her son a token for mankind" (21:91). The Quran teaches that Mary is to be revered because she completely submitted herself to God's will, even though it meant that her own family would accuse her of unchastity when it was discovered that she was pregnant (19:16–21). The Quran also records Jesus as an infant verbally defending Mary's innocence (19:27–34).

Jesus is an important figure in the Quran, which affirms the truth of the teachings of Jesus as found in the Gospels. Like Christians, Muslims believe in the virgin conception of Jesus by God's Spirit. The Quran also records some of Jesus' miracles, including giving sight to the blind, healing lepers, raising the dead, and breathing life into clay birds (5:110). This last miracle is not recorded in the canonical New Testament but does appear in the noncanonical Gospel of Thomas. The Quran also reports Jesus' proclamation of the need to worship God as the only God and his own status as a witness to God (5:116–17).

Muslim and Christian beliefs about Jesus differ in two areas. First, although Muslims believe in the virgin conception and birth of Jesus through an act of God's Spirit, they do not believe that Jesus is the Son of God. They believe that he is one of the long line of righteous prophets and second only to Muhammad in importance (6:83–87). For Muslims, the Christian doctrine of the Trinity represents a form of polytheism, proclaiming belief in three gods rather than one God alone (4:171, 5:17, 5:72–77).

Second, Muslims do not believe in the crucifixion and resurrection of Jesus (4:157–58). They believe that, although it appeared that Jesus was crucified, instead God took Jesus to Himself in a manner similar to what happened to Elijah (3:55, 4:157–589). Muslims do not believe in the Christian doctrine of Original Sin, so there is no theological need for the all-atoning sacrifice of Jesus through his crucifixion and resurrection. Muslims further believe that each of us will be held accountable before God for our own actions and thus responsible for our own salvation. Therefore, we will not be able to rely upon anyone else, not even Jesus or Muhammad, to save us from our sins.

## Do Muslims have a Sabbath like Jews and Christians?

Friday is the Muslim day of congregational worship. It was not traditionally considered a day of rest, but in some Muslim countries today Friday has replaced the Sunday holiday, which was instituted by colonial powers and therefore often seen as a Western, Christian legacy.

In both Muslim and Western countries, congregational prayer (*juma*) in a mosque takes place at noon on Friday. Many Muslims in America arrange to use their lunch hour or a flexible work schedule (coming to work earlier or staying later) in order to attend their hour-long Friday services. (See next question.) Those who cannot do so go to their mosque or Islamic center on Sunday for congregational prayer, religious education classes, and socializing.

## Do Muslims have a weekly worship service?

Muslims gather at a mosque on Friday for the noon congregational prayer (*juma*). Together Muslims of different ages, ethnic groups, and social status stand side by side in straight rows facing the niche in the wall (*mihrab*) that indicates the direction (*qibla*) of the Holy City of Mecca. Men and women worship in separate groups, women behind the men—for reasons of modesty, because prostrations are part of the prayer ritual. Traditionally only men were required to attend the Friday congregational prayer. Increasingly today, however, women attend the service in large numbers. The prayer is led by an *imam* (leader) who stands in front of the congregation.

A special feature of the Friday prayer is a sermon (*khutba*), often delivered from a wooden platform (*minbar*) modeled on the platform used by Muhammad when he gave sermons to his community. The preacher begins by reciting a verse from the Quran and then gives a short talk addressing the affairs and problems of the community, often combining religious advice on social or political issues with commentary based on the Quran's message. Although in mosques with a permanent staff the imam will usually deliver the sermon, any member of the congregation can do so.

## *Do Muslims have religious holidays or holy days?*

Muslims celebrate two great Islamic holidays. The first is Eid al-Fitr, the Feast of the Breaking of the Fast of Ramadan, whose celebration extends for three days. The second holiday, which is the greater of the two, occurs two and a half months after the first and extends for four days. This is the Eid al-Adha, the Feast of Sacrifice, which marks the annual completion of the pilgrimage to Mecca (*hajj*). These holidays represent a religious obligation for Muslims as well as a social celebration.

In America, Eid prayers are observed in every community where Muslims reside, and gatherings to celebrate the occasions are common. In 2001 the U.S. Post Office issued a stamp to commemorate the Eid al-Fitr. Many Muslim children stay home from school to celebrate these festivals, and in some areas school authorities recognize the Eids as holidays for Muslim youngsters, as they recognize the Jewish holidays of Rosh Hashanah and Yom Kippur.

Traditionally, both Eids are occasions for exchanging visits with relatives and friends. As at Christmas celebrations, gifts of money or new clothes are given to children, and special sweets and other foods are served to family and guests.

In many contexts other religious holidays are celebrated, such as the birthday of the Prophet Muhammad and, in Shii Islam, the birthdays of Ali and the Imams. Shii annually commemorate the "passion" of Hussein during a ten-day period of remembering, ritually reenacting, and mourning the last stand of the Imam Hussein and his followers against the army of the caliph. (See page 45, "What is the difference between Sunni and Shii Muslims?")

## *Does Islam have a clergy?*

Islam does not have an ordained clergy or representatives of a church hierarchy in the way that Christianity does. Any Muslim can lead the prayer or officiate at a wedding or burial. In fact, however, historically certain functions came to be filled by a class that took on distinctive forms of dress and authority that are clergy-like. A variety of roles have come to be played by religious scholars and leaders.

In early Islam, pious Muslims from many walks of life also led prayer or became scholars of the Quran and Islamic sciences, but over time many turned these activities into a profession. Every mosque has an *imam*, respected in the community, the one who "stands in front" to lead the prayer and delivers the Friday sermon. In smaller congregations, various members take turns in performing this role. Larger communities have a full-time imam, the chief official who performs the many functions that a priest or rabbi might perform: leading a ritual prayer, administering the mosque or Islamic center or school as well as community activities, visiting the sick, and instructing young people preparing to marry, etc.

Scholars of the Quran, Islamic law, and theology (who are called *ulama*, meaning "the learned") came to represent a permanent class of religious scholars often distinguished in society by their form of dress. They claimed a primary role as the protectors and authoritative interpreters of Islam. Many titles exist for Islamic religious scholars, reflecting their functions in interpreting Islam, some in theology, others in law.

Among the ulama, *mujtahid* is a special title for one who is qualified to interpret Islamic Law (using *ijtihad*, or independent reasoning). A *mufti* is a specialist in Islamic law competent to deliver a *fatwa*, a legal interpretation or judgment. In Sufism (Islamic mysticism), a Sufi master (*pir*) functions as spiritual leader of his followers.

In Sunni Islam, many governments have created the position of Grand Mufti, or senior religious leader. In Shii Islam (the Twelver or Ithna Ashari sect), a hierarchy of religious leaders evolved, at whose apex were Grand Ayatollahs.

In modern times, Islamic reformers include not only the ulama but also educated laity who combine a knowledge of Islam and modern sciences. Today the laity share with the ulama the role of interpreters of Islam.

## What is a mosque?

The word *mosque* comes from the Arabic word *masjid* (place for ritual prostration). The Prophet Muhammad's mosque in Medina, the first Muslim place of worship, functioned as a gathering place for worship, meditation, and learning. Unlike churches or synagogues with their rows of benches or pews, the mosque's main prayer area is a large open space, the expansive floors adorned with oriental carpets. An important feature of the prayer area is the *mihrab*, an ornamental arched niche set into the wall, which indicates the direction of Mecca (which Muslims always face when praying). Next to the mihrab is the *minbar*, a raised wooden platform (similar to a pulpit) modeled after the one that the Prophet Muhammad ascended to give his sermons to the community. The prayer leader delivers his sermon from the steps of the minbar.

Because of the need for cleansing prior to prayer, most mosques have a spot set aside for performing ablutions away from the main prayer area.

The mosque, as the sacred space for individual and congregational worship, has social and intellectual significance for Muslims. Mosques have served as places for prayer, meditation, and learning as well as focal points for the religious and the social life of the Muslim community throughout its history. A mosque's atmosphere is one of tranquility and reflection but also of relaxation. When visiting a mosque, one is as likely to see people chatting quietly or napping on the carpets as praying and reading the Quran.

Historically, wherever Muslims have settled in sufficient numbers, one of their first efforts has been to erect a mosque. In twenty-first-century America, where Islam will soon be the second largest religion, mosque construction has increased exponentially. Over 2,100 mosques and/or Islamic centers, large and small, located throughout the United States in small towns and villages as well as in major cities, are currently serving a diverse American-Muslim community. Many of these mosques incorporate and reflect the diversity of Muslims in America. The membership of others, however, is drawn along ethnic or racial lines. The same phenomenon has been seen in other faiths. For example, one could find two Catholic churches with separate schools, one Irish and one Italian- or French-speaking, across the street from each other. In some places more mosques than might otherwise be needed have been created to accommodate such differences. In some cities and towns one can identify separate Arab, South Asian, Turkish, or African-American mosques.

Mosques have served a multiplicity of functions all over the world. Beyond their use for individual worship and Friday

congregational prayer, they are often the site of Quranic recitations and retreats, especially during Ramadan. They are used
as centers for the collection and distribution of *zakat* (charitable contributions). Many pilgrims visit their local mosques
when they depart for and return from the *hajj* (pilgrimage to
Mecca) and *umrah* (minor pilgrimage). The dead are placed
before the *mihrab* for funerary prayers. Mosques are sometimes the nucleus of an Islamic center housing activities for a
multigenerational, multiethnic Islamic community. (See next
question.) Marriages and business agreements are often contracted in the mosque, and education takes place in various
forms. In times of crisis, worshippers gather for mutual support and to receive guidance from religious leaders.

### What is an Islamic center?

An Islamic center is similar to the Christian and Jewish community centers that have become an integral part of many
churches and synagogues in America and around the world.
For Muslims, it provides a place for prayer as well as a location for social gatherings, community celebrations, and religious classes. In America, many of these community activities
take place on Sunday, when Muslims are free from weekday
work obligations. The center may be a building that stands
alone or part of a mosque complex.

The diverse offering of some American mosques and centers might include youth sports activities, social services such
as job and computer training, job placement, and programs
featuring political candidates. Internationally, mosques and
Islamic centers have also provided the social services that some
governments have failed to offer their citizens.

## Are there any divisions in Islam?

As a world religion, Islam is practiced in diverse cultures in Africa, the Middle East, Asia, Europe, and America. Differences in religious and cultural practices are therefore wide-ranging. Although there are no denominations in Islam such as exist in the Christian faith (Roman Catholic, Methodist, Episcopalian, Lutheran, etc.), like all faiths, Islam has developed divisions, sects, and schools of thought over various issues. While all Muslims share certain beliefs and practices, such as belief in God, the Quran, Muhammad, and the Five Pillars of Islam, divisions have arisen over questions of political and religious leadership, theology, interpretations of Islamic law, and responses to modernity and the West.

The division of opinion about political and religious leadership after the death of Muhammad led to the division of Muslims into two major branches—Sunnis (85 percent of all Muslims) and Shiis (15 percent). (See next question.) In addition, a small but significant radical minority known as the Kharijites should be mentioned. Although they have never won large numbers of followers, their unique theological position has continued to influence political and religious debate up to the present day.

Sunni Muslims believe that because Muhammad did not designate a successor, the best or most qualified person should be either selected or elected as leader (*caliph*). Because the Quran declared Muhammad to be the last of the prophets, this caliph was to succeed Muhammad as the political leader only. Sunnis believe that the caliph should serve as the protector of the faith, but he does not enjoy any special religious status or inspiration.

Shiis, by contrast, believe that succession to the leadership of the Muslim community should be hereditary, passed down to Muhammad's male descendants (descended from Muhammad's daughter Fatima and her husband Ali), who are known as Imams and who are to serve as both religious and political leaders. Shiis believe that the Imam is religiously inspired, sinless, and the interpreter of God's will as contained in Islamic law, but not a prophet. Shiis consider the sayings, deeds, and writings of their Imams to be authoritative religious texts, in addition to the Quran and Sunnah. Shiis further split into three main divisions as a result of disagreement over the number of Imams who succeeded Muhammad. (See page 48, "What are the divisions among Shii Muslims?")

The Kharijites (from *kharaja*, to go out or exit) began as followers of the caliph Ali, but they broke away from him because they believed him to be guilty of compromising God's will when he agreed to arbitrate rather than continue to fight a long, drawn-out war against a rebellious general. After separating from Ali (whom they eventually assassinated), the Kharijites established a separate community designed to be a "true" charismatic society strictly following the Quran and Sunnah of the Prophet Muhammad. The Kharijite world was separated neatly into believers and nonbelievers, Muslims (followers of God) and non-Muslims (enemies of God). These enemies could include other Muslims who did not accept the uncompromising Kharijite point of view. Sinners were to be excommunicated and were subject to death unless they repented. Therefore, a caliph or ruler could only hold office as long as he was sinless. If he fell from this state, he was outside the protection of law and must be deposed or killed. This mentality influenced the famous medieval theologian and legal scholar Ibn Taymiyya (d. 1328) and has been replicated in modern times by Islamic Jihad, the group that assassinated Egypt's President Anwar Sadat, as well as by Osama bin Laden and other extremists who call for the overthrow of "un-Islamic" Muslim rulers.

Differences of opinion about political and religious leadership have led Sunnis and Shiis to hold very different visions of sacred history. Sunnis experienced a glorious and victorious history under the Four Rightly Guided Caliphs and the expansion and development of Muslim empires under the Umayyad and Abbasid dynasties. Sunnis can thus claim a golden age in which they were a great world power and civilization, which they see as evidence of God's guidance and the truth of the mission of Islam. Shiis, on the other hand, struggled unsuccessfully during the same time period against Sunni rule in the attempt to restore the imamate they believed God had appointed. Therefore, Shiis see in this time period the illegitimate usurpation of power by the Sunnis at the expense of creating a just society. Shii historical memory emphasizes the suffering and oppression of the righteous, the need to protest against injustice, and the requirement that Muslims be willing to sacrifice everything, including their lives, in the struggle with the overwhelming forces of evil (Satan) in order to restore God's righteous rule.

Divisions of opinion also exist with respect to theological questions. One historical example is the question of whether a ruler judged guilty of a grave (mortal) sin should still be considered legitimate or should be overthrown and killed. Most Sunni theologians and jurists taught that the preservation of social order was more important than the character of the ruler. They also taught that only God on Judgment Day is capable of judging sinners and determining whether or not they are faithful and deserving of Paradise. Therefore, they concluded that the ruler should remain in power since he could not be judged by his subjects. Ibn Taymiyya was the one major theologian and jurist who made an exception to this position and taught instead that a ruler should and must be overthrown.

Ibn Taymiyya's ire was directed at the Mongols. Despite their conversion to Islam, they continued to follow the Yasa code of laws of Genghis Khan instead of the Islamic law, Shariah. For Ibn Taymiyya this made them no better than the polytheists of the pre-Islamic period. He issued a *fatwa* (formal legal opinion) that labeled them as unbelievers (*kafirs*) who were thus excommunicated (*takfir*). This fatwa established a precedent: despite their claim to be Muslims, their failure to implement Shariah rendered the Mongols apostates and hence the lawful object of jihad. Muslim citizens thus had the right, indeed duty, to revolt against them, to wage jihad. Ibn Taymiyya's opinions remain relevant today because they have inspired the militancy and religious worldview of organizations like Osama bin Laden's al-Qaeda network.

Other examples of divisions over theological questions include arguments over whether the Quran was created or uncreated and whether it should be interpreted literally or metaphorically and allegorically. Historically, Muslims have also debated the question of free will versus predestination. That is, are human beings truly free to choose their own actions or are all actions predetermined by an omniscient God? What are the implications of such beliefs upon human responsibility and justice?

Islamic law provides one of the clearest and most important examples of diversity of opinions. Islamic law developed in response to the concrete realities of daily life. Since the heart of Islam and being a Muslim is submission to God's will, the primary question for believers was "What should I do and how?" During the Umayyad Empire (661–750), rulers set up a rudimentary legal system based upon the Quran, the Sunnah, and local customs and traditions. However, many pious Muslims became concerned about the influence of rulers on the development of the law. They wanted to anchor Islamic law more firmly to its revealed sources and make it less vulnerable to manipulation by rulers and their appointed judges.

Over the next two centuries, Muslims in the major cities of Medina, Mecca, Kufa, Basra, and Damascus sought to discover and delineate God's will and law through the science of jurisprudence. Although each city produced a distinctive interpretation of the law, all cities shared a general legal tradition. The earliest scholars of Islamic law were neither lawyers nor judges nor students of a specific university. They were men who combined professions such as trade with the study of Islamic texts. These loosely connected scholars tended to be gathered around or associated with major personalities. Their schools of thought came to be referred to as law schools.

While many law schools existed, only a few endured and were recognized as authoritative. Today, there are four major Sunni law schools (Hanafi, Hanbali, Maliki, and Shafii) and two major Shii schools (Jafari and Zaydis). The Hanafi came to predominate in the Arab world and South Asia; the Maliki in North, Central, and West Africa; the Shafii in East Africa and Southeast Asia; and the Hanbali in Saudi Arabia. Muslims are free to follow any law school but usually select the one that predominates in the area in which they are born or live.

Perhaps nowhere are the differences in Islam more visible than in the responses to modernity. Since the nineteenth century, Muslims have struggled with the relationship of their religious tradition developed in premodern times to the new demands (religious, political, economic, and social) of the modern world. The issues are not only about Islam's accommodation to change but also about the relationship of Islam to the West, since much of modern change is associated with Western ideas, institutions, and values. Muslim responses to issues of reform and modernization have spanned the spectrum from secularists and Islamic modernists to religious conservatives or traditionalists, "fundamentalists," and Islamic reformists.

Modern secularists are Western oriented and advocate a separation between religion and the rest of society, including politics. They believe that religion is and should be strictly a private matter. Islamic modernists believe that Islam and modernity, particularly science and technology, are compatible, so that Islam should inform public life without necessarily dominating it. The other groups are more "Islamically" oriented but have different opinions as to the role Islam should play in public life. Conservatives, or traditionalists, emphasize the authority of the past and tend to call for a reimplementation of Islamic laws and norms as they existed in that past. "Fundamentalists" emphasize going back to the earliest period and teachings of Islam, believing that the Islamic tradition needs to be purified of popular, cultural, and Western beliefs and practices that have "corrupted" Islam. However, the term *fundamentalist* is applied to such a broad spectrum of Islamic movements and actors that, in the end, it includes both those who simply want to reintroduce or restore their pure and puritanical vision of a romanticized past and others who advocate modern reforms that are rooted in Islamic principles and values. There are a significant number of Islamic reformers, intellectuals, and religious leaders who also emphasize the critical need for an Islamic reformation, a wide-

ranging program of reinterpretation (*ijtihad*) and reform urg-
ing fresh approaches to Quranic interpretation as well as to
issues of gender, human rights, democratization, and legal
reform.

## What is the difference between Sunni and Shii Muslims?

Sunni and Shii Muslims represent the two largest institutional
divisions within the Muslim community. Today, Sunnis constitute approximately 85 percent of Muslims and Shiis make
up 15 percent. The Shii have significant numbers in Iran, Iraq,
Bahrain, and Lebanon. The differences that led to the forma-
tion of these two groups centered on disagreements about
who should be the successor to the Prophet Muhammad.

In the early Muslim community, Muhammad provided im-
mediate and authoritative answers. Muhammad's death in 632
was a traumatic event for the Muslim community, marking
not only the end of direct, personal contact with and guidance
from the Prophet but also the end of direct revelation from
God. The companions of the Prophet moved quickly to steady
and reassure community members. Abu Bakr, the man whom
Muhammad had appointed to lead the Friday communal prayer
in his absence, announced the death of the Prophet in this
way: "Muslims! If any of you has worshipped Muhammad, let
me tell you that Muhammad is dead. But if you worship God,
then know that God is living and will never die!"

The majority of Muslims, who came to be called Sunnis, or
followers of the Sunnah (example) of the Prophet, believed
that Muhammad had died without establishing a system for
selecting a successor or designating a replacement. After an
initial period of uncertainty, the elders or leaders of Medina

selected Abu Bakr to be the *caliph* (successor, deputy). An early convert who had been Muhammad's close companion and trusted advisor as well as his father-in-law, Abu Bakr was respected for his sagacity and piety. Thus Sunni Muslims adopted the belief that leadership should pass to the most qualified person, not through hereditary succession.

As caliph, Abu Bakr became the political and military leader of the community. Although he was not a prophet—the Quran had declared Muhammad to be the last of the prophets—the caliph had religious prestige as head of the community of believers (*ummah*). This was symbolized in later history by the caliph's right to lead the Friday prayer and the inclusion of the caliph's name in the community's prayers.

A minority of the Muslim community, the Shiis, or Party of Ali, opposed the selection of Abu Bakr as caliph, believing that succession should be hereditary. Since Muhammad had no sons who survived infancy, this minority believed that succession should pass through Muhammad's daughter Fatima and that her husband Ali, Muhammad's first cousin and closest living male relative, should be the leader (called Imam) of the Islamic community. Shiis took strong exception to the fact that Ali was passed over for the position of caliph three times, finally gaining his rightful place after thirty-five years only to be assassinated a few short years later. To make matters worse, Ali's charismatic son Hussein, who had been persuaded to lead a rebellion against the caliph Yazid, was overwhelmed and massacred along with his small band of followers.

Muslims point out that the differences between Sunnis and Shiis do not have to do with dogma but rather are political, having to do with the qualifications for the head of the Muslim community. Their shared belief and practice notwithstanding, however, they also developed different views about the meaning of history.

Historically, Sunnis have almost always ruled over Shiis. Because Shiis existed as an oppressed and disinherited minority, they understood history to be a test of the righteous community's perseverance in the struggle to restore God's rule on earth. Realization of a just social order led by their Imam became the dream of Shiis throughout the centuries. While Sunni history looked to the glorious and victorious history of the Four Rightly Guided Caliphs and then the development of imperial Islam under the Umayyads, Abbasids, and Ottomans, Shii history was the theater for the struggle of the oppressed and disinherited. Thus, while Sunnis can claim a golden age when they were a great world power and civilization, which they believe is evidence of God's favor upon them and a historic validation of Muslim beliefs, Shiis see in these same developments the illegitimate usurpation of power by Sunni rulers at the expense of a just society. Shiis view history more as a paradigm of the suffering, disinheritance, and oppression of a righteous minority community who must constantly struggle to restore God's rule on earth under His divinely appointed Imam.

In the twentieth century, Shii history was reinterpreted as a paradigm providing inspiration and mobilization to actively fight against injustice, rather than passively accept it. This reinterpretation has had the most significant impact among the Shiis in Lebanon, who struggled to achieve greater social, educational, and economic opportunities during the 1970s and 1980s, and in Iran, where the Shah was equated with Yazid, and Ayatollah Khomeini and his followers with Hussein, during the Islamic revolution of 1978–79. Thus the victory of the Islamic revolution was declared the victory of the righteous against illegitimate usurpers of power.

## *What are the divisions among Shii Muslims?*

Shii Islam developed three main divisions, stemming from disagreement over the number of Imams who succeeded Muhammad: the Zaydis (also called the Fivers) recognized five Imams, the Ismailis (also called the Seveners) recognized seven, and the Ithna Ashari (also called the Twelvers) recognized twelve. The Zaydis split with the other Shiis by recognizing Hussein's grandson Zayd as the fifth Imam. They believed that any descendant of Ali who was willing to assert his claim to the imamate publicly and fight for it could become Imam. The Zaydis were the first Shii group to achieve independence. They founded a dynasty in Tabaristan on the Caspian Sea in 864. Another Zaydi imamate state was founded in Yemen in 893 and lasted until 1963.

The split between the Ismailis (Seveners) and Ithna Ashari (Twelvers) occurred in the eighth century over the question of who succeeded the sixth Imam, Jafar al-Sadiq (d. 765). The Ismailis recognize seven Imams, ending with Jafar al-Sadiq's son Ismail, who was designated to become the seventh Imam but who predeceased his father and left no son. They formed a revolutionary movement against the Sunni caliphate and established the Fatimid Dynasty, whose empire stretched from Egypt and North Africa to the Sind province of India between the tenth and twelfth centuries.

An Ismaili offshoot, the Nizari Ismailis, were particularly vehement in their violent opposition to Sunni Abbasid rule. Their tactics of violence and terror earned them the epithet of the Assassins. One of the ironies of history is that a Nizari leader who fled to India established a line of Imams known by the honorific title of Agha Khan and created a nonviolent main-stream form of Shii Islam that now has prosperous communities in Canada, Britain, East Africa, and South Asia. The current Harvard-educated Agha Khan oversees the cultural and spiritual lives of his followers, in addition to looking after the educational, social, and commercial institutions of the community.

The third and most populous Shii group, the Ithna Ashari (Twelvers), recognized twelve legitimate successors to Muhammad. Today, they are a majority in Iran, Iraq, and Bahrain. The twelfth Imam, Muhammad al-Muntazar (Muhammad the Awaited One) "disappeared" in 874 as a child with no sons, creating a major dilemma for the line of succession. Shii theology resolved this dilemma with the doctrine of the Hidden Imam, which declares that the twelfth Imam did not die but rather "disappeared" and is in hiding, or "occulation," for an unspecified period of time. This messianic figure is expected to return as the divinely guided Mahdi at the end of time to vindicate his followers, restore his faithful community, and usher in a perfect Islamic society of justice and truth. In the interim, Shiis are guided in religious matters by religious experts, or *mujtahids* (those capable of independently interpreting Islamic law). In contrast to the majority Muslim experience, Twelver Shiism developed a clerical hierarchy at whose apex are religious leaders acknowledged by their followers as *ayatollahs* (signs of God) because of their reputations for knowledge and piety.

## What is Wahhabi Islam?

Until recently, most Westerners had never heard of Wahhabi Islam, but we have now repeatedly heard this term with respect to Osama bin Laden and Saudi Arabia. There are many interpretations of Islam, many schools of theology and law.

Among the most ultraconservative is Wahhabi Islam, the official form of Islam in Saudi Arabia. The Wahhabi movement takes its name from Muhammad Ibn Abd al-Wahhab (1703–1791), a scholar of Islamic law and theology in Mecca and Medina. Disillusioned by the decline and moral laxity of his society, Abd al-Wahhab denounced many popular beliefs and practices as un-Islamic idolatry and a return to the paganism of pre-Islamic Arabia. He rejected blind imitation or following (*taqlid*) of past scholarship. He regarded the medieval law of the *ulama* (religious scholars) as fallible and, at times, unwarranted innovations (*bida*) or heresy. Abd al-Wahhab called for a fresh interpretation of Islam that returned to the "fundamentals" of Islam, the Quran and the Sunnah (example) of the Prophet Muhammad.

Muhammad Ibn Abd al-Wahhab joined with Muhammad Ibn Saud, a local tribal chief, to form a religious-political movement. Ibn Saud used Wahhabism to legitimate his jihad to subdue and unite the tribes of Arabia, converting them to this puritanical version of Islam. Like the Kharijites, Wahhabi theology saw the world in white and black categories—Muslim and non-Muslim, belief and unbelief, the realm of Islam and that of warfare. They regarded all Muslims who did not agree with them as unbelievers to be subdued (that is, fought and killed) in the name of Islam. Central to Muhammad Ibn Abd al-Wahhab's theology was the doctrine of God's unity (*tawhid*), an absolute monotheism reflected in the Wahhabis' self-designation as "Unitarians" (*muwahiddun*)—those who uphold the unity of God. In imitation of Muhammad's destruction of the pantheon of pre-Islamic tribal gods in Mecca's sacred shrine (Kaaba) and its restoration to worship of the one true God (Allah), Wahhabi puritanism spared neither the sacred tombs of Muhammad and his Companions in Mecca and Medina nor the Shiite pilgrimage site at Karbala (in modern Iraq) that housed the tomb of Hussein. The destruction of this venerated site has never been forgotten by Shii Muslims and contributed to the historic antipathy between the Wahhabi of Saudi Arabia and Shii Islam in both Saudi Arabia and Iran. Centuries later, many would point to Wahhabi-inspired iconoclasm as the source behind the Taliban's wanton destruction of Buddhist monuments in Afghanistan, an action condemned by Muslim leaders worldwide.

In the early nineteenth century, Muhammad Ali of Egypt defeated the Saudis, but the Wahhabi movement and the House of Saud proved resilient. By the early twentieth century, Abdulaziz Ibn Saud recaptured Riyadh, united the tribes of Arabia, restored the Saudi kingdom, and spread the Wahhabi movement. The Kingdom of Saudi Arabia melded the political and religious in a self-declared Islamic state, using the Wahhabi interpretation of Islam as the official basis for state and society.

Internationally, the Saudis, both government-sponsored organizations and wealthy individuals, have exported their ultraconservative version of Wahhabi Islam to other countries and communities in the Muslim world and the West. They have offered development aid, built mosques, libraries, and other institutions, funded and distributed religious tracts, and commissioned imams and religious scholars. Wahhabi puritanism and financial support have been exported to Afghanistan, Pakistan, the Central Asian Republics, China, Africa, Southeast Asia, the United States, and Europe. At the same time, some wealthy businessmen in Saudi Arabia and the Gulf have provided financial support to extremist groups who follow a militant "fundamentalist" brand of Islam (commonly referred to as Wahhabi or Salafi) with its jihad culture.

The challenge is to distinguish between the export of an ultraconservative theology on the one hand and militant extremism on the other. This difficulty is compounded by the propensity of authoritarian governments in Central Asia and China, especially since 9/11, to use the label "Wahhabi extremism" for all opposition, legitimate and illegitimate, and thus justify widespread repression of all opposition to their rule and policies.

## Is there a difference between Muslims and Black Muslims?

African-American Islam emerged in the early twentieth century when a number of black Americans converted to Islam, the religion that they believed was part of their original African identity. Islam was preferred over Christianity, which was seen as a religion of white supremacy and oppression, the religion of those who treated black Americans as second-class citizens and denied them their full civil rights. By contrast, Islam seemed to emphasize a brotherhood of believers, the *ummah*, which transcended race and ethnicity.

In the early 1930s Wallace D. Fard Muhammad drew on the Quran and the Bible to preach a message of black liberation in the ghettos of Detroit. Wallace D., who was called the Great Mahdi, or messiah, taught withdrawal from white society, saying that blacks were not Americans and owed no loyalty to the state. He rejected Christianity and the domination of white "blue-eyed devils" and emphasized the "religion of the Black Man" and the "Nation of Islam."

Fard mysteriously disappeared in 1934. Elijah Muhammad (formerly Elijah Poole [1897–1975]) took over and built the "Nation of Islam," an effective national movement whose members became known as "Black Muslims." Elijah Muhammad denounced white society's political and economic oppression of blacks and its results: self-hatred, poverty, and dependency. His apocalyptic message promised the fall of the white racist oppressor America and the restoration of the righteous black community, a "Chosen People." His religious teachings gave alienated and marginalized poor and unemployed people a sense of identity and community and a program for self-improvement and empowerment. Elijah Muhammad emphasized a "Do for Self" philosophy, appealing particularly to black youth, focusing on black pride and identity, strength and self-sufficiency, strong family values, hard work, discipline, thrift, and abstention from gambling, alcohol, drugs, and pork. By the 1970s the Nation of Islam had more than one hundred thousand members.

A number of basic beliefs in the Black Muslim movement differed significantly from mainstream Islam. Elijah Muhammad announced that Wallace D. Fard was Allah, and thus that God was a black man, and that he, Elijah Muhammad, not the Prophet Muhammad, was the last messenger of God. The Nation taught black supremacy and black separatism, not Islam's brotherhood of all believers in a community that transcends racial, tribal, and ethnic differences. In addition, the Nation did not follow the Five Pillars of Islam or observe major Muslim rituals.

A key individual who rose through the ranks of the Nation of Islam to gain national prominence was Malcolm X, who accepted the teaching of the Nation of Islam while in prison. Drawn by Elijah Muhammad's black nationalism, denunciation of white racism, and promotion of self-help, Malcolm Little became Malcolm X: ex-smoker, ex-drinker, ex-Christian, and ex-slave. The "X" also represented the unknown surname of Malcolm X's slave ancestors, preferred to a name originally given by a slave owner. A gifted, charismatic speaker, Malcolm was the most visible and prominent spokesperson for Elijah Muhammad, recruiting new members (including the boxer Cassius Clay, renamed Muhammad Ali), establishing temples, and preaching the message of the Nation of Islam nationally and internationally. However, Malcolm's exposure to world events and contact with Sunni Muslims resulted in a gradual change in his own religious worldview, away from that of Elijah Muhammad and toward mainstream Islam.

In 1964, Malcolm X left the Nation of Islam to start his own organization. At this time he also went on pilgrimage to Mecca. On the pilgrimage he was deeply affected by what he experienced—the equality of all believers regardless of race, tribe, or nation. Malcolm explained his realization that "we were truly all the same (brothers)—because their belief in one God removed the 'white' from their minds, the 'white' from their behavior and the 'white' from their attitude." He also recognized that he did not know how to perform Islam's daily prayers and had not observed the other prescribed practices in the Five Pillars of Islam. Malcolm returned from the pilgrimage as El Hajj Malik El-Shabazz, a Muslim, rather than a Black Muslim, and he changed his position on black nationalism, moving to pan-Africanism, which aligns African Americans with their cultural and religious ties in Africa.

On February 21, 1965, the former Malcolm X was assassinated as he spoke to an audience in New York City. Two members of the Nation of Islam were convicted of the murder.

The 1960s were a time of transition for the Nation of Islam. Not only Malcolm X but also Wallace D. Muhammad, son of Elijah Muhammad, along with his brother Akbar Muhammad, a distinguished scholar of Islam who had studied in Egypt and Scotland, questioned and challenged some of the teachings and strategies of their father. Both sons were excommunicated by their father. Yet toward the end of his life Elijah Muhammad also made the pilgrimage to Mecca and began to modify some of his teachings. By the time of his death in 1975, Elijah Muhammad and the Nation were publicly acknowledged for their constructive contributions to America's inner cities and communities.

When Wallace D. Muhammad succeeded his father as Supreme Minister of the Nation, he implemented major reforms in doctrines and organizational structure, so that they conformed to the teachings of orthodox Sunni Islam. Wallace Fard was identified as the founder of the Nation and Elijah Muhammad as the leader who brought black Americans to his interpretation of Islam. Wallace Muhammad made the pilgrimage to Mecca and encouraged his followers to study Arabic in order to better understand Islam. Temples were renamed mosques, and their leaders were now called imams rather than ministers. The community observed the Five Pillars of Islam in union with the worldwide Islamic community to which they now belonged. Black separatist doctrines were dropped as the Nation community began to participate within the American political process. Finally, the equality of male and female members was reaffirmed, and women were given more responsible positions in the ministry of the community. While the Nation continued to work for social and economic change, business ventures were cut back and religious identity and mission were given priority.

At the end of the 1970s Wallace transferred organizational leadership to an elected council of six imams and focused on his role as religious and spiritual leader. In the mid-1980s, signaling his and the Nation's new religious identity and mission, Wallace changed his name to Warith Deen Muhammad and renamed the community American Muslim Mission, integrating it within the global mainstream Islamic community and within the American Muslim community.

Media coverage of the Black Muslim movement often focuses on Louis Farrakhan, the man who led a minority of Nation members in protest against Warith's reforms. Farrakhan bitterly rejected the changes instituted by both Malcolm and Warith Deen Muhammad, maintaining that only he and his followers had remained faithful to the original message and mission of Elijah Muhammad. Farrakhan retained the mantle of leadership of the Nation of Islam, along with its black nationalist and separatist doctrines. Farrakhan's strident, separatist messages as well as the international connections he has established with militant leaders like those of Libya and Iran have given him and his minority of followers a disproportionate visibility.

Farrakhan's militancy and anti-Semitic statements have been widely criticized. At the same time, his charisma and energy directed to fighting crime and drugs and to rehabilitating prisoners have earned praise for the Nation. His leadership of the 1995 Million Man March in Washington, D.C., received widespread media coverage and support from Christian as well as Muslim leaders and organizations. In recent years, Farrakhan has moved the Nation closer to more orthodox Islamic practices, maintaining a closer identity with mainstream Islam.

### Are Sufis Muslims?

Yes. Sufis belong to the mystical tradition of Islam known as Sufism. The name "Sufi" is derived from the Arabic word *suf* (wool), in honor of the coarse woolen garments worn by the first Sufis, resembling the garb of Christian monks and mystics in other faiths. Like other mystical movements in Christianity, Judaism, Hinduism, and Buddhism, the Sufi path seeks to discipline the mind and body in order to experience directly the presence of God. Sufis view their struggle to find God as one that takes place in the world, in contrast to the Christian monastic tradition of withdrawing from the world in order to find God.

Sufis set as their highest priority the individual spiritual effort of self-sacrifice and discipline in a struggle within oneself against greed, laziness, and ego. This struggle is known as the "greater jihad" (as opposed to the "lesser jihad" of armed struggle in the defense of Islam). This "greater jihad" is carried out by devoting oneself completely to fulfilling God's will, studying and meditating on the Quran and the Sunnah (the example of Muhammad), performing religious duties, especially prayer and fasting, focusing on the centrality of God and the Last Judgment, denying material desires that could distract one from God, and carrying out good works. A famous woman mystic, Rabia al-Adawiyya (d. 801), added the devotional love of God to Sufi practices.

Like Islamic law, Sufism began as a reform movement in response to the growing materialism and wealth of Muslim society that accompanied the expansion and growing power of the Islamic empire. While some believed that strict adherence to Islamic law and rituals was the solution to the excesses of imperial lifestyles and luxuries, Sufis found the emphasis on laws, rules, duties, and rights to be spiritually lacking. Instead, they emphasized the "interior" path, seeking the purity and simplicity of the time of Muhammad, as the route to the direct and personal experience of God. Following the example of Muhammad in working tirelessly in the world to create the ideal Islamic society, Sufis have often played an important role in the political life of Muslims. For example, in the eighteenth and nineteenth centuries, Sufi brotherhoods led jihad movements (the Mahdi in Sudan, Fulani in Nigeria, and Sanusi in Libya) that spearheaded an Islamic revivalist wave that regenerated society, created Islamic states, and fought off colonial powers.

The Sufi orders also played an important role in the spread of Islam through missionary work. Their tendency to adopt and adapt to local non-Islamic customs and practices in new places and their strong devotional and emotional practices helped them to become a popular mass movement and a threat to the more orthodox religious establishment. In this way, Sufism became integral to popular religious practices and spirituality in Islam. However, their willingness to embrace local traditions also left them open to criticism by the conservative religious establishment for being unfaithful to the tenets of Islam. Indeed, popular Sufism at times slipped into magic and superstition, as well as withdrawal from the world. Some of the major Islamic revival and reform movements of the eighteenth, nineteenth, and twentieth centuries sought to eliminate superstitious practices from Sufism and bring it back into line with more orthodox interpretations of Islam.

Sufism today exists throughout the Muslim world and in a variety of devotional paths. It remains a strong spiritual presence and force in Muslim societies, in both private and public life, and enjoys a wide following in Europe and America, attracting many converts to Islam.

### Who are these Islamic fundamentalists?

The term *Islamic fundamentalism* evokes many images: the Iranian revolution, the World Trade Center and Pentagon attacks of 9/11, the Ayatollah Khomeini, Osama bin Laden and al-Qaeda, suicide bombers. For many, this term is simply equated with radicalism, religious extremism, and terrorism. But images of hostage crises, embassies under siege, hijackings, and bombings lead to simplistic understandings. The term *fundamentalist* is applied to such a broad spectrum of Islamic movements and actors that in the end it includes both those who simply want to reintroduce or restore their pure and puritanical vision of a romanticized past and others who advocate modern reforms that are rooted in Islamic principles and values.

The ranks of Islamic fundamentalists include those who provide much-needed services to the poor such as schools, health clinics, and social welfare agencies, as well as extremists. For every country where Islamic militants seek to reach their goals through violence and terrorism, there are Islamic political parties and social welfare organizations that participate in national and local elections and function effectively within mainstream society.

Though convenient, the use of the term *fundamentalism*, which originated in Christianity, can be misleading in the Islamic context, where it has been applied to a broad and diverse group of governments, individuals, and organizations. The conservative monarchy of Saudi Arabia, the radical socialist state of Libya, clerically governed Iran, the Taliban's Afghanistan, and the Islamic Republic of Pakistan have all been called "fundamentalist." The term obscures their differences. Libya and Iran, for example, have in the past espoused many anti-Western views, while Saudi Arabia and Pakistan have often been close allies of the United States. *Political Islam* and *Islamism* are more useful terms when referring to the role of Islam in politics.

Islamic fundamentalism, or political Islam, is rooted in a contemporary religious resurgence, which began in the late 1960s and has affected both the personal and public life of Muslims. On the one hand, many Muslims have become more religiously observant, demonstrating increased attention to prayer, fasting, dress, and family values as well as renewed interest in Islamic mysticism, or Sufism. On the other, Islam reemerged in public life as an alternative political and social ideology to secular nationalism, Western capitalism, and Marxist socialism, which many believe had failed to help the majority of Muslims escape poverty, unemployment, and political oppression. Governments, Islamic movements, and organizations from moderate to extremist have appealed to Islam for legitimacy and to mobilize popular support.

Islamic activists—"fundamentalists"—both extremists and mainstream come from very diverse educational and social backgrounds. They are recruited not only from the poor and unemployed living in slums and refugee camps but also from the middle class in prosperous neighborhoods. While some are from economically or politically marginalized or "oppressed" backgrounds, others are well-educated university students and professionals. Many hold degrees in the sciences, education, medicine, law, or engineering—professionals who function in and contribute to their societies.

Many Islamic activists are part of a nonviolent political and social force in mainstream society. Activists have served as prime minister of Turkey, president and speaker of the national assembly in Indonesia, and deputy prime minister of Malaysia, as well as cabinet officers, parliamentarians, and mayors in countries as diverse as Egypt, Sudan, Turkey, Iran, Lebanon, Kuwait, Yemen, Jordan, Pakistan, Bangladesh, Malaysia, Indonesia, and Israel-Palestine.

At the same time, a militant minority are religious extremists and terrorists: Sheikh Omar Abdel Rahman, a religious leader who was imprisoned for his involvement in plans to bomb major sites in the United States, has a doctorate in Islamic studies; Osama bin Laden, a university graduate and member of one of the wealthiest families in Saudi Arabia, became a global terrorist and leader of al-Qaeda; Ayman al-Zawahiri, right-hand man to Osama bin Laden, is a trained surgeon from a prominent Egyptian family.

## *Is Islam medieval and against change?*

Islam and much of the Muslim world are often seen as medieval for many reasons: cultural (for example, the existence of strong patriarchal societies and the veiling and seclusion of women), political (authoritarianism on the one hand and fundamentalism on the other) and economic (lack of development and failed economies).

Yet, in truth, today as in the past Muslims interpret Islam in many different ways. Like their Abrahamic brothers and sisters, Muslims exhibit a wide range of approaches and orientations, ranging from ultraconservative and fundamentalist to progressive or reformist.

The contrast between Islam and Christianity and Judaism appears as more vivid because we usually equate Christianity and Judaism with believers in modern Europe and America rather than those in more traditional, premodern, and less developed societies such as Ethiopia, Eritrea, or Sudan. Ethiopian Jews and Christians, whose religion is linked to local tribal and cultural traditions, also contrast sharply with their Western cobelievers. Such contrasts are of course more evident among Christianity's 1.5 billion adherents spread across the globe than among Judaism's 14 to 18 million followers, who have a far more restricted geographic representation.

The forces of tradition and the authority of the past have been reinforced in Islam by a variety of historic forces and experiences. For four centuries (the seventeenth through the twentieth), much of the Islamic world was dominated by European colonialism. Religions, like countries, under "siege" tend to focus on survival, preserving and protecting what they have, rather than seeking and accepting change. Thus Islamic calls for reform are often labeled by opponents as simply attempts to Westernize Islam.

When conservatives try to preserve Islam, they often do not distinguish between revealed sources of faith and socially conditioned human interpretations historically preserved in manuals of Islamic law and theology. In contrast, reformers stress the difference between divinely mandated beliefs, practices, and laws and human interpretations from the past as they engage in a bold process of reinterpretation and reform that reapplies Islamic guidelines to problems in the modern world.

Amidst these differing religious interpretations and orientations, change has occurred and continues to occur in a process that sometimes seems to take two steps forward and one step back. Secular and religious reformers have promoted changes affecting religious understanding and education, family laws (marriage, divorce, and inheritance), broader opportunities for women's education and employment, democratization, pluralism, and human rights. On the other hand, more conservative voices among religious leaders as well as some ultraconservative Islamic activists and organizations have often attempted to implement or impose rigid, militant, puritanical, and intolerant beliefs, values, and attitudes.

Finally, many authoritarian governments (secular and religious) use religion to restrict freedom of thought and expression. They limit or prohibit an independent press, media, political parties, and trade unions in the name of religion.

Muslims today are at a critical crossroads. They are faced with making radical social, political, and economic changes that the Western world has had many decades to implement gradually. Amidst increasing globalization, Muslims strive to survive and compete, often with limited resources, and to preserve their identity in a world dominated (culturally as well as politically and economically) by the West. For many, the role of religion is critical in the preservation of their personal and national identities. It provides a sense of continuity between their Islamic heritage and modern life. For some, the temptation is to cling to the authority and security of the past. Others seek to follow new paths, convinced that their faith and a tradition of Islamic reform that has existed throughout the ages can play a critical role in restoring the vitality of Muslim societies.

## Is Islam compatible with modernization?

The Muslim world is popularly pictured as lacking development. While some attribute this to Islam, lack of development in the Muslim world, as elsewhere, is in fact primarily due to issues of economy, limited resources, and education rather than religion. In Muslim societies around the world today, it is evident that modernization is seen as a goal worthy of pursuit and implementation. Travelers are often surprised to see television antennae or satellite dishes even in the remotest villages. The skylines of major cities are dotted with their World

Trade Centers, modern factories, and corporations. People—secular and conservative, fundamentalists and reformers—equally take advantage of modern technology: cell phones, computers, the Internet, fax machine, automobiles, and planes. The absence of certain technologies such as the Internet in some Muslim countries is due not to resistance from the people but to cost or security concerns (the fears of authoritarian rulers that the Internet will take away their control).

Belief in an inherent conflict between Islam and modernization has arisen when modernization is equated with the Westernization and secularization of society. One Western expert said that Muslims must choose between Mecca and mechanization, implying that modernization necessarily threatened and eroded faith. This attitude reflects a belief that faith and reason, religion and science, are ultimately incompatible. Thus to become modern intellectually, politically, and religiously would mean a loss or watering down of faith, identity, and values.

Secular Muslims and Islamic activists exist side by side in societies and in the professions. Their opposing views regarding the relationship of religious belief to society and politics do give rise to conflict. If some believe that a viable modern nation-state requires a separation of religion and politics, or mosque and state, others advocate governments and societies that are more informed by Islamic principles and values. Yet as examples from around the Muslim world (Egypt, Turkey, Malaysia, Indonesia) and other countries such as Japan or China have demonstrated, modernization does not have to mean the wholesale Westernization or secularization of society. Nowhere is this clearer than among so-called fundamentalists, or Islamic activists, who are also graduates of modern universities, majoring in science, medicine, law, engineering, journalism, business, and the social sciences. Many hold prominent positions in their respective professions, functioning effectively and contributing to the ongoing modernization of their societies.

## *Are there any modern Muslim thinkers or reformers?*

Because acts of violence and terrorism grab the headlines, most of us know a lot more about advocates of a "clash," militant jihadists, than about those who are working toward a peaceful revolution and civilizational dialogue. Nevertheless, today Islam's encounter with the West and the need for Islamic reform are being addressed by intellectuals, religious leaders, and activists all over the world.

Like Islamic modernist movements in the early twentieth century and, later, the Islamic ("fundamentalist") movements of the Muslim Brotherhood in Egypt and the Jamaat-i Islami in Pakistan, today's Islamically oriented intellectuals and activists are continuing the process of Islamic modernization and reform. They represent a creative new stage, a minority who are not only reformulating Islam but also implementing their ideas through their work in government and other public arenas.

The reformist and modernist Muslim Abdurrahman Wahid, former leader of Indonesia's Nahdatul Ulama (Renaissance of Religious Scholars) movement with thirty million members, became the first democratically elected president of Indonesia; Dr. Amien Rais, the University of Chicago–trained political scientist and former leader of Indonesia's Muhamaddiyya movement, became speaker of Indonesia's national assembly; Anwar Ibrahim, founder of ABIM, Malaysia's Islamic Youth

Movement, went on to become the deputy prime minister of Malaysia; Dr. Ecmettin Erbakan, a trained engineer, became Turkey's prime minister; and Muhammad Khatami, a religious scholar, was president of Iran. Many Islamically motivated professionals serve in parliaments or as mayors of major cities and are leaders in their professions (lawyers, physicians, engineers, and scientists).

Reformist thought is especially prevalent in America and Europe, where there is a free and open environment absent in many Muslim countries. In Europe we find Muslim scholars and activists like Drs. Tariq Ramadan, grandson of Hasan al-Banna, founder of Egypt's Muslim Brotherhood, a Swiss academic and activist, and Muhammad Arkoun of the Sorbonne university in Paris. In America, they include Drs. Sayyid Hossein Nasr of George Washington University, an expert on Sufism and on Islam and science; Abdulaziz Sachedina of the University of Virginia, who has written extensively on Islam and democratization and human rights; Howard University's Sulayman Nyang, a prolific author who writes about Islam in America and Africa; Fathi Osman, who has written extensively on the Quran, pluralism, and Islamic reform; Amina Wadud of Virginia Commonwealth University, author of *Quran and Woman*; Amira el-Azhary Sonbol of Georgetown University, an expert on women and law; and Khaled Abou El Fadl of UCLA Law School, who addresses issues of Islam, law, pluralism, gender, and violent extremism. These scholars formulate and debate new ideas, develop rationales and strategies for reform, and train the next generation in a more dynamic, progressive vision. Increasingly, their influence and impact are felt not only in the West but also in Muslim countries, as their ideas are exported through translations of their works.

Today, a two-way information superhighway spans the world. Ideas come not only from the traditional centers of

Islamic scholarship in Muslim countries but also from religious scholars, leaders, and institutions in the West and from their students, who return to become professionals and leaders in their home countries. The Internet plays host to debates between progressive Muslims and more conservative voices globally, providing a venue for heated discussion of Islam's relationship to the state, Islamic banking, democracy, religious and political pluralism, family values, and gay rights, among many other topics.

Just as they were in the process of modern reform in Judaism and Christianity, questions of leadership and the authority of the past (tradition) are critical in Islamic reform. "Whose Islam?" is a major question. Who reinterprets, decides, leads, and implements change? Is it rulers and regimes, the vast majority of whom are unelected kings, military, and former military, or should it be elected parliaments? Is it the *ulama* (religious scholars) or clergy, who continue to see themselves as the primary interpreters of Islam, although many are ill prepared to respond creatively to modern realities? Or are Islamically oriented intellectuals and activists with a modern education most qualified? Too often in authoritarian societies that restrict freedom of thought and expression, and thus effective leadership, extremists like Osama bin Laden with their theology of confrontation and hate fill the vacuum.

The second major question is "What Islam?" Is Islamic reform simply a restoration of past doctrines and laws, or is it a reformation through a reinterpretation and reformulation of Islam to meet the demands of modern life? While some call for an Islamic state based upon the reimplementation of classical formulations of Islamic laws, others argue the need to reinterpret and reformulate that law in light of the new realities of contemporary society.

The process of Islamic reform is difficult. As in all religions, tradition—centuries-old beliefs and practices—is a powerful force, rooted in the claim of being based upon the teachings of the Quran or the practice (Sunnah) of the Prophet. The vast majority of religious scholars and local mosque leaders (*imams*) and preachers, who wield significant influence over the religious education and worldview of the majority of Muslims, are products of a more traditional religious education. The ideas of a vanguard of reformers will never have broad appeal and acceptance unless they are incorporated within the curricula of seminaries and schools and universities where religion is taught. A twofold process of reform, intellectual and institutional, will be required in the face of powerful conservative forces, limited human and financial resources, and a culture of authoritarianism that limits or controls freedom of thought in many countries.

# ISLAM AND OTHER RELIGIONS

## Do Muslims believe Islam is the only true religion?

Islam, like Christianity, is a global religion with a universal mission, calling all of humankind to worship the one true God. Historically, Muslims have believed that God sent his revelation one final time to Muhammad and the Muslim community and that they have an obligation to spread the faith: "We have sent you only to proclaim good news and to warn all mankind" (Quran 34:28).

Islam teaches that, although God first made a covenant with Moses and the Jews, and then with Jesus and Christians, God made a final covenant with Muhammad and the Muslim community. While the Quran and Muslim belief acknowledge that God sent many prophets and messengers, Muslims, like Jews and Christians before them, believe that they possess the fullness of God's message and truth and that other faiths have an imperfect, corrupted, and distorted version. Muslims believe that because Muhammad received God's final and complete revelation to humankind, they have a universal message and mission, to call all humankind to worship the one true God.

From earliest times, Muslims of all walks of life have therefore engaged in propagating their faith (*dawa*, the call) wherever they went. Merchants as well as religious leaders and soldiers spread the faith as the Islamic community expanded politically. As in the past, today many Muslims stand ready to be a witness to their faith through preaching, writing, example, and providing financial support to build mosques and schools, publish materials on Islam, and assist those agencies that seek to convert non-Muslims.

## Is Islam intolerant of other religions?

Despite the recent example of the Taliban in Afghanistan and sporadic conflicts between Muslims and Christians in Sudan, Nigeria, Pakistan, and Indonesia, theologically and historically Islam has a long record of tolerance.

The Quran clearly and strongly states that "there is to be no compulsion in religion" (2:256) and that God has created not one but many nations and peoples. Many passages underscore the diversity of humankind. The Quran teaches that God deliberately created a world of diversity (49:13): "O humankind, We have created you male and female and made you nations and tribes, so that you might come to know one another." Muslims, like Christians and Jews before them, believe that they have been called to a special covenant relationship with God, constituting a community of believers intended to serve as an example to other nations (2:143) in establishing a just social order (3:110).

Moreover, Muslims regard Jews and Christians as "People of the Book," people who have also received a revelation and a scripture from God (the Torah for Jews and the Gospels for Christians). The Quran and Islam recognize that followers of the three great Abrahamic religions, the children of Abraham, share a common belief in the one God, in biblical prophets such as Moses and Jesus, in human accountability, and in a

Final Judgment followed by eternal reward or punishment. All share the common hope and promise of eternal reward: "Surely the believers and the Jews, Christians and Sabians [Middle East groups traditionally recognized by Islam as having a monotheistic orientation], whoever believes in God and the Last Day, and whoever does right, shall have his reward with his Lord and will neither have fear nor regret" (2:62).

Historically, while the early expansion and conquests spread Islamic rule, Muslims did not try to impose their religion on others or force them to convert. As "People of the Book," Jews and Christians were regarded as protected people (*dhimmi*), who were permitted to retain and practice their religions, be led by their own religious leaders, and be guided by their own religious laws and customs. For this protection, they paid a poll or head tax (*jizya*). While by modern standards this treatment amounted to second-class citizenship in premodern times, it was very advanced. No such tolerance existed in Christendom, where Jews, Muslims, and other Christians (those who did not accept the authority of the pope) were subjected to forced conversion, persecution, or expulsion. Although the Islamic ideal was not followed everywhere and at all times, it existed and flourished in many contexts.

In recent years, religious intolerance has become a major issue in self-styled Islamic governments in Saudi Arabia, Afghanistan under the Taliban, Iran, and Sudan, as well as in the actions of religious extremist organizations from Egypt's Islamic Jihad to Osama bin Laden and al-Qaeda who have been intolerant toward not only non-Muslims but also other Muslims who do not accept their version of "true Islam." The situation is exacerbated in some countries where Muslims have clashed with Christians (Nigeria, the Philippines, and Indonesia), Hindus (India and Kashmir), and Jews (Israel). These confrontations have sometimes been initiated by the Muslim community and sometimes by the Christian. In some cases it becomes difficult to distinguish whether conflicts are driven primarily by politics and economics or by religion. Finally, more secular governments in Egypt, Tunisia, Turkey, Syria, and elsewhere have often proven to be intolerant of mainstream Islamic organizations or parties that offer an alternative vision of society or are critical of government policies.

From Egypt to Indonesia and Europe to America, many Muslims today work to reexamine their faith in the light of the changing realities of their societies and their lives, developing new approaches to diversity and pluralism. Like Jews and Christians before them, they seek to reinterpret the sources of their faith to produce new religious understandings that speak to religious pluralism in the modern world. The need to redefine traditional notions of pluralism and tolerance is driven by the fact that in countries such as Egypt, Lebanon, Pakistan, India, Nigeria, Malaysia, and Indonesia, Muslims live in multireligious societies, and also by new demographic realities. Never before have so many Muslim minority communities existed across the world, in particular in America and Europe. The specter of living as a permanent minority community in non-Muslim countries has heightened the need to address and redefine questions of pluralism and tolerance. Like Roman Catholicism in the 1960s, whose official acceptance of pluralism at the Second Vatican Council was strongly influenced by American Catholics' experience as a minority, Muslim communities in America and Europe are now struggling with their questions of identity and assimilation.

Reformers emphasize that diversity and pluralism are integral to the message of the Quran, which teaches that God created a world composed of different nations, ethnicities, tribes, and languages: "To each of you We have given a law and a way and a pattern of life. If God had pleased He could surely have made you one people [professing one faith]. But He wished to try and test you by that which He gave you. So try to excel in good deeds. To Him will you all return in the end, when He will tell you how you differed" (5:48). Many point to the example of the Prophet and his community at Medina. The Constitution of Medina accepted the coexistence of Muslims, Jews, and Christians. Muhammad discussed and debated with, and granted freedom of religious thought and practice to, the Jews and Christians, setting a precedent for peaceful and cooperative interreligious relations. Many challenge the exclusivist religious claims and intolerance of Islamic groups who believe that they alone possess the "true" interpretation of Islam and attempt to impose it on other Muslims and non-Muslims alike. In many ways, Islam today is at a crossroads as Muslims, mainstream and extremist, conservative and progressive, struggle to balance the affirmation of the truth of their faith with the cultivation of a pluralism and tolerance rooted in mutual respect and understanding.

## How is Islam similar to Christianity and Judaism?

Judaism, Christianity, and Islam, in contrast to Hinduism and Buddhism, are all monotheistic faiths that worship the God of Adam, Abraham, and Moses—creator, sustainer, and lord of the universe. They share a common belief in the oneness of God (monotheism), sacred history (history as the theater of God's activity and the encounter of God and humankind), prophets and divine revelation, angels, and Satan. All stress moral responsibility and accountability, Judgment Day, and eternal reward and punishment.

All three faiths emphasize their special covenant with God, for Judaism through Moses, Christianity through Jesus, and Islam through Muhammad. Christianity accepts God's covenant with and revelation to the Jews but traditionally has seen itself as superseding Judaism with the coming of Jesus. Thus Christianity speaks of its new covenant and New Testament. So, too, Islam and Muslims recognize Judaism and Christianity: their biblical prophets (among them Adam, Abraham, Moses, and Jesus) and their revelations (the Torah and the Gospel, or Message of Jesus). Muslim respect for all the biblical prophets is reflected in the custom of saying "Peace and blessings be upon him" after naming any of the prophets and in the common usage of the names Ibrahim (Abraham), Musa (Moses), Daoud (David), Sulayman (Solomon), and Issa (Jesus) for Muslims. In addition, Islam makes frequent reference to Jesus and to the Virgin Mary, who is cited more times in the Quran than in the New Testament.

However, Muslims believe that Islam supersedes Judaism and Christianity—that the Quran is the final and complete word of God and that Muhammad is the last of the prophets. In contrast to Christianity, which accepts much of the Hebrew Bible, Muslims believe that what is written in the Old and New Testaments is a corrupted version of the original revelation to Moses and Jesus. Moreover, Christianity's development of "new" dogmas such as the belief that Jesus is the Son of God and the doctrines of redemption and atonement is seen as admixing God's revelation with human fabrication.

Peace is central to all three faiths. This is reflected historically in their use of similar greetings meaning "peace be upon you": *shalom aleichem* in Judaism, *pax vobiscum* in Christianity, and *salaam alaikum* in Islam. Often, however, the greeting of peace has been meant primarily for members of one's own faith community. Leaders of each religion, from Joshua and King David to Constantine and Richard the Lion-Hearted to Muhammad and Saladin, have engaged in holy wars to spread or defend their communities or empires. The joining of faith and politics continues to exist in modern times, though manifested in differing ways, as seen in Northern Ireland, South Africa, America, Israel, and the Middle East.

Islam is similar to Judaism in its emphasis on practice rather than belief, on law rather than dogma. The primary religious discipline in Judaism and Islam has been religious law; for Christianity it has been theology. Historically, in Judaism and Islam the major debates and disagreements have been among scholars of religious law over matters of religious practice, whereas in Christianity the early disputes and cleavages in the community were over theological beliefs: the nature of the Trinity or the relationship of Jesus' human and divine natures.

## How do Muslims view Judaism? Christianity?

Both Jews and Christians hold a special status within Islam because of the Muslim belief that God revealed His will through His prophets, including Abraham, Moses, and Jesus.

> Say, We believe in God, and in what has been revealed to us, and in what has been sent down to Abraham and Ismail and Isaac and Jacob and their offspring, and what has been revealed to Moses and Jesus and to all the prophets of our Lord. We make no distinction between them and we submit to Him and obey. (Quran 3:84)

The Quran and Islam regard Jews and Christians as children of Abraham and refer to them as "People of the Book," since all three monotheistic faiths descend from the same patri-lineage of Abraham. Jews and Christians trace themselves back to Abraham and his wife Sarah; Muslims, to Abraham and his servant Hagar. Muslims believe that God sent his revelation (Torah) first to the Jews through the prophet Moses and then to Christians through the prophet Jesus. They recognize many of the biblical prophets, in particular Moses and Jesus, and those are common Muslim names. Another common Muslim name is Mary. In fact, the Virgin Mary's name occurs more times in the Quran than in the New Testament; Muslims also believe in the virgin birth of Jesus. However, they believe that over time the original revelations to Moses and Jesus became corrupted. The Old Testament is seen as a mixture of God's revelation and human fabrication. The same is true for the New Testament and what Muslims see as Christianity's devel-opment of "new" and erroneous doctrines such as that Jesus is the Son of God and that Jesus' death redeemed and atoned for humankind's original sin.

## Why do Muslims persecute Christians in Muslim countries?

Religious conflict and persecution historically and today ex-ist across the religious spectrum: Hindu fundamentalists have clashed with Muslims, Christians, and Sikhs in India, Chris-tian Serbs with Muslim Bosnians and Kosovars, Jews with Pal-estinian Muslims and Christians, Tamil (Hindu) with Sinhalese (Buddhist) in Sri Lanka, Christians with Muslims in Lebanon, Catholics with Protestants in Northern Ireland.

   History teaches us that religion is a powerful force that has been used for good and for ill. From Egypt, Sudan, and Nige-ria to Pakistan, Indonesia, and the southern Philippines, Muslims have clashed with Christians. Moreover, despite an impressive record of religious pluralism in the past, the situation in Southeast Asia has gotten worse rather than better. It is often difficult to identify specific conflicts as motivated primarily by religion as opposed to politics or economics.

It is useful to recall that historically Islam's attitude toward other religions, especially Judaism and Christianity, was more tolerant than that of Christianity. However, Muslim-Christian relations have deteriorated over time under the influence of conflicts and grievances, from the Crusades and European colonialism to contemporary politics. Part of the legacy of colonialism is a deep-seated belief, nurtured by militant religious leaders, that indigenous Christians were favored by and benefited from colonial rule or that they are the product of the European missionaries and their schools that converted local Muslims.

The situation is compounded in areas where Christians proved more affluent or successful. The creation of the state of Israel and subsequent Arab-Israeli wars and conflicts have contributed to a deterioration of relations between Palestinan Muslims and Christians and Israeli Jews. Anti-Semitism, like anti-Arab and anti-Islamic attitudes, has grown among a significant sector.

In recent decades, conservative and fundamentalist interpretations of Islam (as well as the Christianity preached by leaders like Pat Robertson, Franklin Graham, and Jerry Falwell) have been sources of intolerance, persecution, violence, and terrorism. Local religious leaders who espouse and preach an exclusivist and militant view of religion raise generations of narrow-minded believers who, given the right circumstances, will take to the streets and engage in intercommunal or intersectarian battles. This has led to the torching of churches and mosques in Nigeria and Indonesia, the bombing of Christian churches in Pakistan, and the slaughter of Christians in Egypt and the southern Philippines. The rise of fundamentalism has brought with it intolerant theologies of hate that have led groups like Islamic Jihad and the Gammaa Islamiyya in Egypt or Laskhar Jihad in Indonesia to attack Christians. Christians have suffered under self-styled Islamic governments in Sudan and Pakistan. "Islamic laws" such as Pakistan's blasphemy law have been used to imprison and threaten Christians with the death penalty.

As previously noted, however, often the main sources of conflict are political and economic rather than religious. The civil war in Lebanon, which shattered the celebrated Lebanese multireligious mosaic, is one example. Lebanon's government had been established on the basis of proportional representation tied to a 1932 census in which Christians, especially Maronite Christians, predominated, followed by Sunni, Shii, and Druze. The president was a Maronite Christian, the prime minister a Sunni Muslim, and so forth. Positions in government, the bureaucracy, and the military were distributed according to which religious sect or community one belonged to. Changing demographics led many Muslim leaders and groups to call for a redistribution of power and wealth.

At the heart of the conflict in Israel-Palestine is the creation of the state of Israel and the Palestinian demand for a Palestinian state and the right to return to their lands. At the same time, for a significant minority of Muslims and Jews, the struggle is at its heart based upon conflicting religious claims to the land. Similarly, for some among the Muslim minority in the southern Philippines, autonomy or statehood has become a rallying cry against the Christian-dominated government in Manila, whose historic practice of moving Christians from the north to the south is regarded as an unacceptable occupation of Muslim lands. In Malaysia and Indonesia, the significant economic prosperity and power of the Chinese minority, many of whom are Christian and who constitute an extremely small percentage of the population, have been and continue to be sources of resentment and conflict.

The long struggle of Christian East Timor for independence from Muslim Indonesia is another example. This conflict, though it had a religious dimension, was primarily about political independence for the former Portuguese colony. The government of Indonesia was hardly motivated by religion in its policies toward East Timor. Finally, the long civil war between North and South in Sudan has often been cast as a conflict between the Arab Muslim North and the Christian South. Actually, the majority of the South is animist, though many of the military leaders are Christian. More important, although there is a religious dimension and Christians have suffered persecution under Sudan's "Islamic" government, the struggle has been political and economic (over control of the South's oil reserves) as much as religious.

## *Haven't Jews and Christians always been enemies of Islam?*

The relationship of Jews and Christians to Islam, like the relationship of Christianity to Judaism, is long and complex, conditioned by historical and political realities as well as religious doctrine. Jewish and Christian tribes lived in Arabia at the time of the Prophet Muhammad. Jews and Christians were members or citizens of the early Muslim community at Medina.

In his early years, Muhammad anticipated that Jews and Christians, as "People of the Book," would accept his prophetic message and be his natural allies. The Quran itself confirms the sending of prophets and revelation to Jews and Christians and recognizes them as part of Muslim history: "Remember, we gave Moses the Book and sent him many an apostle; and to Jesus, son of Mary, We gave clear evidence of the truth, reinforcing him with divine grace" (23:49–50; see also 5:44–46, 32:23, 40:53).

Muhammad initially presented himself as a prophetic reformer reestablishing the religion of Abraham. For example, like the Jews, the Muslims initially faced Jerusalem during prayer and fasted on the tenth day of the lunar month. Muhammad made a special point of reaching out to the Jewish tribes of Medina. The Jews of Medina, however, had political ties to the Quraysh tribe of Mecca, so they resisted Muhammad's overtures. Shortly afterward, Muhammad received a revelation changing the direction of prayer from Jerusalem to Mecca, marking Islam as a distinct alternative to Judaism.

When Muhammad consolidated his political and military control over Medina, he wrote and promulgated documents commonly referred to as the Constitution of Medina (c. 622–624), which regulated social and political life. The constitution states that the believers comprise a single community, or *ummah*, which is responsible for collectively enforcing social order and security and for confronting enemies in times of war and peace. Tribes remained responsible for the conduct of their individual members, and a clear precedent was set for the inclusion of other religions as part of the broader community led by Muslims. The Jewish population was granted the right to internal religious and cultural autonomy, including the right to observe Jewish religious law, in exchange for their political loyalty and allegiance to the Muslims.

Muslims point to the Constitution of Medina as evidence of Islam's inherent message of peaceful coexistence, the permissibility of religious pluralism in areas under Muslim rule, and the right of non-Muslims to be members of and participants in the broader Muslim community. However, relations between the early Muslim community and some Jewish tribes became strained when the Jews backed Muhammad's Meccan rivals. Judged as traitors for their support of his enemies, many were attacked and killed. This confrontation became part of the baggage of history and would continue to influence the attitudes of some Muslims in later centuries. Recently, this legacy can be seen in official statements from Hamas and Osama bin Laden. Both not only condemn Jews for Israeli occupation and policies in Palestine but also see the current conflict as just the most recent iteration of an age-old conflict dating back to the Jews' "rejection and betrayal" of Islam and the Prophet's community at Medina.

Nevertheless, in many Muslim communities at various times in history, Jews found a home where, as "People of the Book," or *dhimmi*, they lived, worked, and often thrived. Vibrant Jewish communities existed in Muslim countries like Egypt, Morocco, Turkey, and Iran. When the Catholic rulers Ferdinand and Isabella drove the Jews out of Spain, many found refuge in North Africa and the Ottoman Empire. The establishment of the state of Israel was a turning point in relations between Muslims and Jews. The political fallout from the struggle between the Palestinians and Zionism severely strained Jewish-Muslim relations in Muslim countries. As a result, the majority of Jews emigrated or fled to Israel and other parts of the world.

The relationship of Christians and Muslims is even more complex. Despite common theological roots, Islam and Christianity were in contention from the outset. Islam offered an alternative religious and political vision. Just as Christians saw their faith as superseding the covenant of the Jews with God, Islam now declared that God had made a new covenant, revealing his word one final and complete time to Muhammad, the "seal" or final prophet. Islam, like Christianity, proclaimed a universal message and mission and thus challenged the claims of Christianity. Moreover, the remarkable spread of Islam, with its conquest of the eastern (Byzantine) wing of the Roman Empire, challenged the political power and hegemony of Christendom.

The history of Christianity and Islam has been one of both conflict and coexistence. When Muslims conquered Byzantium, they were welcomed by some Christian sects and groups, who were persecuted as heretics by "official" Christianity, that is, Catholicism. Many Christians welcomed a Muslim rule that gave them more freedom to practice their faith and imposed lighter taxes. Despite initial fears, the Muslim conquerors proved to be far more tolerant than imperial Christianity had been, granting religious freedom to indigenous Christian churches and Jews.

This spirit was further reflected in the tendency of early Islamic empires to incorporate the most advanced elements from surrounding civilizations, including Byzantine and Persian Sasanid imperial and administrative practices and Hellenic science, architecture, art, medicine, and philosophy. Christians like John of Damascus held positions of prominence in the royal courts. Christian and Jewish subjects assisted their Muslim rulers with the collection and translation of the great books of science, medicine, and philosophy from both East and West.

However, the rapid expansion of Islam also threatened Christian Europe, as Muslims seemed poised to sweep across

Europe until finally turned back by Charles Martel in southern France in 732. The Crusades, the Inquisition, and European colonialism represented major periods of confrontation and conflict, as did the rise and expansion of the Ottoman Empire into Europe.

The most often cited example of interreligious tolerance in history is that of Muslim rule in Spain (al-Andalus) from 756 to about 1000, which is usually idealized as a period of interfaith harmony, or *convivencia* (living together). Muslim rule of Spain offered the Christian and Jewish populations seeking refuge from the class system of Europe the opportunity to become prosperous small landholders. Christians and Jews occupied prominent positions in the court of the caliph in the tenth century, serving as translators, engineers, physicians, and architects. The Archbishop of Seville commissioned an annotated translation of the Bible for the Arabic-speaking Christian community.

Islamic history also contains positive examples of interfaith debate and dialogue, beginning in the time of Muhammad. Muhammad himself had engaged in dialogue with the Christians of Najran, resulting in a mutually agreeable relationship whereby the Najranis were permitted to pray in the Prophet's mosque. The fifth Sunni caliph, Muawiyyah (ruled 661–669), regularly sent invitations to the contending Jacobite and Maronite Christians to come to the royal court to discuss their differences. Debates involving both Muslims and Jews occurred in Spanish Muslim courts, and a sixteenth-century interreligious theological discussion between Catholic priests and Muslim clerics was presided over by the Mughal Emperor Akbar. These debates were not always conducted between "equals" (indeed, many were held precisely in order to "prove" that the other religion was "wrong," as was also the case for dialogues initiated by Christians). The fact that the debate was permitted and encouraged, however, indicates some degree of open exchange between faiths, a significant stage of educational and cultural achievement in the Muslim world.

During the Crusades, despite their conflict, Muslims tolerated the practice of Christianity—an example that was not emulated by the other side. In the thirteenth century some treaties between Christians and Muslims granted Christians free access to sacred places then reoccupied by Islam. The great Christian saint Francis of Assisi met the Muslim leader Salah al-Din's nephew Sultan al-Malik al-Kamil in 1219. The sultan granted freedom of worship to his more than thirty thousand Christian prisoners when hostilities were suspended, as well as offering them the choice of returning to their own countries or fighting in his armies. Furthermore, Muslims maintained an open-door policy to Jews escaping from persecution in Christian Europe during the Inquisition.

The Ottoman Empire is a prime example of the positive treatment of religious minorities in a Muslim majority context. The Ottomans officially recognized four religiously based communities, known as *millets*: Greek Orthodox, Armenian Gregorian, Muslim, and Jewish. Under the millet system, Islam assumed the prime position, but each other millet was placed under the authority of its own religious leaders and permitted to follow its own religious laws. The millet system enabled the empire to accommodate religious diversity, placing non-Muslims in a subordinate position to Muslims and offering them protected status. Members of minority religions further had the right to hold government positions in some cases. Thus, a limited form of religious pluralism and tolerance were important components of Ottoman statecraft.

In the contemporary era, religious and political pluralism has been a major issue in the Muslim world. Many of those seeking to establish Islamic states in the Muslim world look to historical precedents to determine the status of non-Muslims. Although many call for a strict reinstatement of the gradations of citizenship that accompanied dhimmi status in the past, others recognize that this approach is not compatible with the pluralistic realities of the contemporary world and international human rights standards.

Those who advocate gradation of citizenship according to religious affiliation believe that an Islamic state, defined as one in which Islamic law is the law of the land, must necessarily be run by Muslims because only Muslims are capable of interpreting Islamic law. This has been the position of Islamization programs in Pakistan, the Sudan, Afghanistan, and Iran, which have legislated that only Muslims have the right to hold senior government positions. Obviously, this is not satisfactory to non-Muslims who wish to enjoy full and equal rights of citizenship. Religious minorities have in fact been persecuted and subject to discrimination under some Muslim governments in countries like the Taliban's Afghanistan, Pakistan, and Sudan. Thus many reformers who do not agree with the application of this classical tradition in modern times insist that non-Muslims be afforded full citizenship rights.

Advocates of reform maintain that pluralism is the essence of Islam as revealed in the Quran and practiced by Muhammad and the early caliphs, rather than a purely Western invention or ideology. They point to the Islamic empires that permitted freedom of religion and worship and protected the dhimmis as evidence of the permissibility and legality of pluralism. While many militants and mainstream conservative or traditionist Muslims advocate classical Islam's dhimmi or the millet system, reformers call for a reinterpretation or reunderstanding of pluralism. Recognizing the need to open the one-party and authoritarian political systems that prevail in the Muslim world, many mainstream Islamists (as distinguished from extremists) also began applying the word *pluralism* to the political process. Since the 1990s, the term has been used to legitimate multiparty systems as well as modern forms of religious pluralism and tolerance.

# CUSTOMS AND CULTURE

## *Why does Islam separate men and women?*

Many, though not all, Muslim societies practice some gender segregation—the separation of men and women—to various degrees, in public spaces such as mosques, universities, and the marketplace. Thus in many mosques men and women have separate areas for prayer or are separated by a screen or curtain. Unmarried men do not mix with unmarried women outside of very specific contexts, such as family gatherings or a meeting between two potential spouses that occurs in the presence of a chaperone. Seclusion, which differs from the public segregation of the sexes, is the practice of keeping women within the home so that they have no contact with public space. Although gender segregation and seclusion are practiced in some Muslim societies, in many Muslim countries, from Egypt and Tunisia to Malaysia and Indonesia, men and women, especially in cities and towns, increasingly study and work together. In our modern, globalizing world, where two incomes are often necessary to maintain a household, women are increasingly joining the workforce and breaking down traditional notions of gendered space.

The practice of separation has both religious and cultural origins. The Prophet's Medina did not practice sexual segregation. Although an integral part of the community, because of their special status, Muhammad's wives were told by the Quran, "O wives of the Prophet! You are not like any of the other women. If you fear God, do not be complaisant in speech so that one in whose heart is a sickness may covet you, but speak honorably. Stay with dignity in your homes and do not display your finery as the pagans of old did" (33:32–33). The Quran later tells Muhammad's wives to place a barrier between themselves and unrelated males. Muslim men are told, "And when you ask [his wives] for anything you want, ask them from before a screen. That makes for greater purity for your hearts and for theirs" (33:53).

There have been many debates about how these verses concerned with modesty and segregation should be interpreted with respect to Muslim women in general. Modern scholars have pointed out that they specifically address only the wives of the Prophet rather than all of womankind. They maintain that until the modern age jurists relied primarily on Prophetic traditions (*hadith*), as well as the belief that women are a source of temptation (*fitnah*) for men, to support women's segregation. In recent decades, more ultraconservative/fundamentalist Muslim leaders, sometimes influenced and supported by Wahhabis (see page 49, "What is Wahhabi Islam?"), have maintained that the verses addressing the wives of the Prophet apply to all Muslim women, who are supposed to emulate the behavior of Muhammad's wives.

However, opinions today vary about the necessity of separation of the sexes. While many believe that the absolute separation of the sexes is unnecessary, many others believe that modesty requirements can be met through appropriate dress and limiting interaction with unrelated males to conversations such as those concerning professional and educational matters, since men and women attend both work and school in mixed company. This holds true even in the religious realm, since women have come to play an important role in mosques, where they not only attend services and pray with men but also teach Quran classes, run independent auxiliaries, and run for and hold elected offices. Several Muslim countries (Pakistan, Bangladesh, Turkey, and Indonesia) have had women prime ministers or presidents.

## Are women second-class citizens in Islam?

The status of women in Muslim countries has long been looked to as evidence of "Islam's" oppression of women in matters ranging from the freedom to dress as they please to legal rights in divorce. The true picture of women in Islam is far more complex.

The revelation of Islam raised the status of women by prohibiting female infanticide, abolishing women's status as property, establishing women's legal capacity, granting women the right to receive their own dowry, changing marriage from a proprietary to a contractual relationship, and allowing women to retain control over their property and to use their maiden name after marriage. The Quran also granted women financial maintenance from their husbands and controlled the husband's free ability to divorce.

The Quran declares that men and women are equal in the eyes of God; man and woman were created to be equal parts of a pair (51:49). The Quran describes the relationship between men and women as one of "love and mercy" (30:21). Men and women are to be like "members of one another" (3:195), like each other's garment (2:187).

Men and women are equally responsible for adhering to the Five Pillars of Islam. Quran 9:71-72 states, "The Believers, men and women, are protectors of one another; they enjoin what is just, and forbid what is evil; they observe regular prayers, pay zakat and obey God and His Messenger. On them will God pour His mercy: for God is exalted in Power, Wise. God has promised to Believers, men and women, gardens under which rivers flow, to dwell therein." This verse draws added significance from the fact that it was the last Quran verse to be revealed that addressed relations between men and women. Some scholars argue on the basis of both content and chronology that this verse outlines the ideal vision of the relationship between men and women in Islam—one of equality and complementarity.

Most Islamic societies have been patriarchal, and women have long been considered to be the culture-bearers within these societies. Prior to the twentieth century, the Quran, *hadith* (traditional stories of the Prophet), and Islamic law were interpreted by men in these patriarchal societies, and these interpretations reflect this environment. Women were not actively engaged in interpreting the Quran, hadith, or Islamic law until the twentieth century. Since then, however, reformers have argued that Quranic verses favoring men need reinterpretation in light of the new social, cultural, and economic realities of the twentieth and twenty-first centuries.

Women have been assigned second-class status in Islam based upon Quran 4:34, which says, "Men have responsibility for and priority over women, since God has given some of them advantages over others and because they should spend their wealth [for the support of women]." However, contemporary scholars have noted that the "priority" referred to in this verse is based upon men's socioeconomic responsibilities for women. It does not say women are incapable of managing their own affairs, controlling themselves, or being leaders.

Nowhere in the Quran does it say that all men are superior to, preferred to, or better than all women. God's expressed preference for certain individuals in the Quran is based upon their faith, not their gender.

Quranic interpretation is at the center of many debates. Some note that the Quran itself specifically distinguishes between two types of verses: those that are universal principles and those that were responding to specific social and cultural contexts or questions and were subject to interpretation (3:7). They believe that those verses that assign greater rights to men (such as 2:223 and 2:228) reflect a patriarchal context in which men were dominant and solely responsible for supporting women. Today, rather than being interpreted literally, these verses should be reformulated to reflect the interests of public welfare. Reformers further argue that gender equality is the intended order established by God, because God does not make distinctions based upon gender in matters of faith.

However, Muslims who advocate a literal interpretation of the Quran believe that the gender inequalities it prescribes apply to every time and place as God's revealed social order. Biology is often used as a justification; because only women can bear children, they argue, the man must provide for and maintain the family so that the woman can do her job of bearing and raising children.

Another apparent example of second-class status for women appears in the Quranic stipulation (2:282) that two female witnesses are equal to one male witness. If one female witness errs, the other can remind her of the truth: "And call to witness two of your men; if two men are not available then one man and two women you approve of, so that if one of them is confused, the other would remind her." Over time, this was

interpreted by male scholars to mean that a woman's testimony should always count for one-half of the value of a man's
testimony. Contemporary scholars have revisited this question also, offering several observations about the sociohistori-
cal context in which the verse was revealed.

First, the verse specifies that witnessing is relevant in cases
of a written transaction, contract, or court case. At the time
the Quran was revealed, most women were not active in business or finance. A woman's expertise in these fields would
most likely have been less than a man's. Another interpretation argues that the requirement for two female witnesses to
equal the testimony of one man was based upon the concern
that male family members might pressure a woman into tes-
tifying in their favor.

Some contemporary female scholars have argued that the
requirement of two female witnesses demonstrates the need
for women to have access to education, both secular and religious, in order to receive the training and experience to be
equal to men in a business environment—something that is
not prohibited by the Quran. In light of the right of women
to own property and make their own investments, this interpretation is in keeping with broader Quranic values.

The Quran counsels compassion and tolerance as well as
mediation in divorce and stresses that spouses "be generous
towards one another" (2:237). Ideally, divorce is a last resort,
discouraged rather than encouraged as reflected in a tradition of the Prophet, "of all the things permitted, divorce is
the most abominable with God." However, historically this
ideal has been undermined and compromised by realities of
patriarchal societies so that divorce rather than polygamy has
been the more serious social problem. This situation has been
compounded by the fact that women have been unable to

exercise their rights either because they were unaware of them or because of pressures in a male dominated society. In many Muslim countries, modern reforms have been introduced to limit a husband's rights and expand those of women. However these reforms have been limited and challenged by more conservative and fundamentalist forces.

The twenty-first century has brought numerous significant reforms for women's rights in both the public and the private spheres. In the overwhelming majority of Muslim countries, women have the right to public education, including at the college level. In many countries, they also have the right to work outside of the home, vote, and hold public office. Particularly notable in recent years have been reforms in marriage and divorce laws.

Among the most important of these reforms have been the abolition of polygamy in some countries and its severe limitation in others, expanded rights for women seeking divorce, including the right to financial compensation, expanded rights for women to participate in contracting their marriage and to stipulate conditions favorable to them in the marriage contract, the requirement that the husband provide housing for his divorced wife and children as long as the wife holds custody over the children, raising the minimum age for marriage for both spouses, prohibiting child marriage, and expanding the rights of women to have custody over their older children.

## What kinds of roles did women play in early Islam?

Women played important roles in the early Muslim community and in the life of Muhammad. Historical and other evidence indicates that a woman (Muhammad's wife Khadija) was the first to learn of the Quranic revelation. Moreover, she owned her own business, hired Muhammad, and later proposed to him. This precedent led jurists to recommend that women could propose to men if they so desired. Women fought in battles and nursed the wounded during the time of the Prophet. They were consulted about who should succeed Muhammad after his death. Women also contributed to the collection and compilation of the Quran and played an important role in the transmission of numerous *hadith* (prophetic traditions).

The fact that women prayed regularly along with men in the mosque is also evidence of their equality in public life during the early period of Islam. Women in the early Muslim community owned and sold property, engaged in commercial transactions, and were encouraged to seek and provide educational instruction. Many women were instructed in religious matters in Muhammad's own home. Muhammad's daughter Fatima, his only surviving child, played a prominent role in his community. She was the wife of Imam Ali and mother of Imams Hussein and Hassan, immaculate and sinless, the pattern for virtuous women and object of prayer and petition. Like her son Hussein she embodies a life of dedication, suffering, and compassion. Muhammad's wife Aisha also played a unique role in the community, as an acknowledged authority on history, medicine, poetry, and rhetoric, as well as one of the most important transmitters of hadith.

In political affairs, women independently pledged their oath of allegiance (*bayah*) to Muhammad, often without the knowledge or approval of male family members, and in many cases distinguished women converted to Islam before the men in their family. The second caliph, Umar Ibn al-Khattab, appointed women to serve as officials in the marketplace of

Medina. The Hanbali school of law (see page 139, "What is Islamic law?") supports the right of women to serve as judges. The Quran holds up the leadership of the Queen of Sheba as a positive example (27:23–44). Rather than focusing on gender, the Quranic account of this queen describes her ability to fulfill the requirements of her office, her purity of faith, her independent judgment, and her political skills, portraying a woman serving as an effective political leader.

## Why do Muslim women wear veils and long garments?

The word *veiling* is a generic term used to describe the wearing of loose-fitting clothing and/or a headscarf. The Quran emphasizes modesty, although there is no specific prescription for covering one's head. The custom of veiling is associated with Islam because of a passage that says, "Say to the believing women that they should lower their gaze and guard their modesty. They should draw their veils over their bosoms and not display their beauty" (24:31). Specific attire for women is not stipulated anywhere in the Quran, which also emphasizes modesty for men: "Tell the believing men to lower their gaze and be modest" (24:30).

The Islamic style of dress is known by many names (*hijab, burqa, chador,* etc.; see glossary for descriptions) because of the multitude of styles, colors, and fabrics worn by Muslim women in countries extending from Morocco to Iran to Malaysia to Europe and the United States, and because of diverse customs and interpretations of the Quranic verses.

Veiling of women did not become widespread in the Islamic empire until three or four generations after the death of Muhammad. Veiling was originally a sign of honor and distinction. During Muhammad's time, the veil was worn by Muhammad's wives and upper-class women as a symbol of their status. Generations later, Muslim women adopted the practice more widely. They were influenced by upper- and middle-class Persian and Byzantine women, who wore the veil as a sign of their rank, to separate themselves not from men but from the lower classes. The mingling of all classes at prayer and in the marketplace encouraged use of the veil among urban Muslim women.

The veil is often seen as a symbol of women's inferior status in Islam. Opponents link veiling with backwardness and oppression and Western dress with individuality and freedom. Critics of veiling, Muslim and non-Muslim, stress the importance of self-expression, which they associate with the distinctive way in which a woman dresses and wears her hair. They believe that any person or religion or culture that requires a mature woman to dress in a certain way infringes on her rights and freedom. They question those who say the veil is for women's protection and ask why not put the burden on the men to control themselves.

Supporters of veiling explain that they choose to wear hijab because it provides freedom from emphasis on the physical and from competing with other women's looks as well as from being sex objects for males to reject or approve. It enables women to focus on their spiritual, intellectual, and professional development. Some scholars have argued that in returning to Islamic dress, particularly in the 1980s, many Muslim women were attempting to reconcile their Islamic tradition with a modern lifestyle, redefining their identities as modern Muslim women. Islamic dress is also used as a sign of protest and liberation. It has developed political overtones, becoming a source of national pride as well as resistance to Western dominance (cultural as well as political) and to authoritarian regimes. Many young Muslim women have adopted Islamic dress to symbolize a return to their cultural roots and rejection of a Western imperialist tradition that in their view shows little respect for women. These young women think that Western fashions force women into uncomfortable and undignified outfits that turn them into sexual objects lacking propriety and dignity. Women who wear Islamic dress thus find it strange or offensive for people to condemn their own modest fashions as imprisoning and misogynist. The West should condemn not the hijab or Islam, they say, but rather a social system that promotes an unrealistic ideal, makes young girls obsessive about their physical beauty and their weight, and teaches young boys to rate girls on the basis of that ideal.

Western and Muslim critics of Islamic dress, on the other hand, question those who say it is their free choice to wear the veil. They see such women as under the sway of an oppressive patriarchal culture or as just submitting to the dictates of their religion. They also say that after seeing the hijab used to control and segregate women, as in Afghanistan under the Taliban, the rest of the world perceives the veil as a symbol of conformity and confinement that reflects on any woman who wears it.

Some Muslims, however, would say that Western women only believe they are free. They do not see how their culture exploits them when they "choose" to spend countless hours on their appearance, wear uncomfortable skin-tight clothes and dangerous high-heeled shoes, and allow themselves to be displayed as sexual objects to sell cars and shaving cream and beer. These Muslims say that Westerners condemn the veil because they themselves are not free to choose.

Since the 1970s, a significant number of "modern" women from Cairo to Jakarta have turned or returned to wearing Islamic dress. Often this is a voluntary movement led by young, urban, middle-class women, who are well educated and work in every sector of society. New fashions have emerged to reflect new understandings of the status and role of women. Indeed, designing contemporary Islamic dress has become a profitable enterprise. Some Muslim women have started their own companies specializing in the design and marketing of fashionable and modest outfits featuring varied flowing garments and matching veils.

Women who wear the scarf complain that, instead of asking what the hijab means to them, people simply assume that veiled women are oppressed. This assumption, they say, oppresses Muslim women more than any manner of dress ever could. Even if a woman wearing the veil is strong and intelligent, her value is automatically discounted by many people who are reluctant to get to know her or invite her to participate in activities. They point out that women of many other cultures and religions—Russian women, Hindu women, Jewish women, Greek women, and Catholic nuns—often wear head coverings. They ask why these women are not viewed as oppressed. If opponents assume that women of other cultures who cover their heads are liberated, why can't they imagine freedom for Muslim women who wear a veil? Muslim women often talk about what the hijab symbolizes: religious devotion, discipline, reflection, respect, freedom, and modernity. But too often nobody asks them what the scarf means to them.

### Why aren't women allowed to work or drive in Islam?

Rather than consider that women's status in the Muslim world might reflect the continued strength of patriarchy, people often assume that Islam is particularly misogynist. If some blame Islam for the oppression of women, however, others see it as a beacon of light and reform.

Restrictions on women's driving (only Saudi Arabia bans women from driving cars) or working (they are legally permitted to work in most Muslim countries) are country specific and very diverse. These restrictions originate not from Islam but rather from cultural customs sometimes wrongly justified under an Islamic banner. The ability to work or drive has little to do with Islam and a lot to do with culture or cultural interpretations of Islam. Fortunately, such restrictions are the clear exception rather than the rule.

The status of women in Muslim countries differs as much as the countries themselves. For several decades women in Muslim societies have been part of an erratic and vacillating process of change that creates many contradictions. For example, women have been prime ministers in Bangladesh, Turkey, and Pakistan and president in Indonesia, and yet in other contexts rights and roles are restricted.

In Saudi Arabia women are sexually segregated and required to be fully covered in public. At the same time, there are more women than men in universities; Saudi women own their own companies and are major landowners. In Egypt, there is no required dress code, and women in Western as well as Islamic dress are visible in every sector of society from education and business to medicine, law, engineering, and government. In Iran, women are required to wear a scarf and *chador* or long coat in public, but they function in a sexually mixed society where they constitute the majority in universities, hold professional positions, and serve in parliament; there is also a woman vice president in the Islamic Republic of Iran. Women in Malaysia have access to the best education, hold responsible professional positions in virtually every sector, and are seen riding motorcycles as frequently as men. In Kuwait, women hold responsible positions in many areas but have not been able to get the vote. Pakistani women vote and have served as ambassador to the United States and in the highest position as prime minister, but they also suffer— particularly the poor and powerless—under "Islamic" laws that restrict their rights in marriage, divorce, and inheritance.

While women in most societies have access to education and employment, they continue to face obstacles and challenges as they seek gender equality and forge new paths in defining their roles in society.

### Why do Muslim men wear turbans or caps?

Not all Muslim men wear turbans, and not all men who wear turbans are Muslims. Sikhs, for example, wear turbans as a religious requirement. Many Muslim men do not wear any head covering at all. Head coverings tend to be associated with culture, rather than necessarily with religion.

Head coverings for Muslim males who choose to wear them include turbans, fez, prayer caps or skullcaps, keffiyahs, and traditional Arab head coverings. Turbans are most often associated with the Taliban of Afghanistan and Iranian clerics. The color of the turban often indicates the status of the wearer: black marks the wearer as a *sayyid*, or descendant of Muhammad, while white signifies that the wearer is not a descendant of Muhammad. The fez was the traditional head covering of Turkish men during the late Ottoman era. It was forcibly replaced with a European-style brimmed hat in the early twentieth century. Keffiyahs tend to be associated with Jordan and

Palestine and are often worn today to indicate sympathy for the Palestinian national cause. Traditional Arab head coverings, such as those worn in Saudi Arabia, were originally designed to protect the head and neck from the sun. Prayer caps and skullcaps are typically found in Pakistan and among some African-American Muslims.

## Why do Muslim men wear beards?

Many Muslim men wear beards in honor of the Prophet Muhammad, who had a beard. Some believe that the beard should be left untrimmed in the style of Muhammad, but many do not accept this assertion; thus differing styles of beards abound, ranging from full beards covering the entire jaw and cheeks to neatly trimmed goatees covering only the chin area. Only in Afghanistan under the Taliban regime were men absolutely required to wear full, untrimmed beards.

Many other Muslim men do not wear beards and do not believe it is a religious requirement. Some who live in Muslim countries that repress any form of Islamic activism or fundamentalism do not wear them because they are more likely to be subject to suspicion and arrest if they do. Some in the West, particularly post–September 11, avoid wearing a beard because bearded Muslim men tend to be more closely associated with extremism.

## Does Islam require circumcision?

As in Judaism, circumcision for males is required in Islam according to both tradition and Muhammad's example (Sunnah). Many Muslims believe that circumcision is required for male converts to Islam. Symbolically, circumcision represents the religious process of submission to God's will and commands and the submission of base passions to the higher spiritual requirements of Islam. In other words, the physical modification of the male organ symbolizes submission of even sexual matters to God.

Socially, circumcision is an important rite of passage for boys and, when carried out at the age of ten or twelve, marks the transition to adulthood and the assumption of male responsibilities, including regular attendance at public prayer. Furthermore, a male who is circumcised at an older age is no longer permitted to mingle as freely with unrelated women.

In the Middle East, the ritual of circumcision is typically carried out somewhere between the ages of two and twelve. In many Muslim countries, the occasion of circumcision is a celebratory event paralleling wedding rituals, including the bringing of gifts and feasting. In Europe and the United States, circumcisions are typically done in the hospital immediately after birth.

Female circumcision is neither an Islamic practice nor is it widespread among Muslims. Rather, it appears to be an African tradition that remains in practice in countries like the Sudan and Egypt, among Muslims and non-Muslims alike.

## Can Muslim men have more than one wife?

The practice of polygamy, or more correctly polygyny (marriage to more than one wife), is a controversial subject in Islamic societies. Many modern Islamic nations have either outlawed or strictly regulated polygamy in a variety of ways (requiring a court review and approval, requiring a wife's permission, etc.). Although polygamy is practiced in some Muslim societies, the vast majority of Muslims today are monogamous.

Although it is found in many religious and cultural traditions, we tend to identify polygamy or polygyny particularly with Islam. In fact, historically polygyny was practiced in Semitic societies in general and Arab culture in particular. It was common among the nobles and leaders in Arabian society and, although less common, can also be seen in biblical Judaism; Abraham, David, and Solomon all had multiple wives.

Polygamy was common in pre-Islamic Arabia; marriage was uncontrolled. A man could have as many wives as he wanted; women were considered inferior, had no rights, and were treated like servants. Seventh-century Arabia was the scene of frequent tribal wars and combat. When men were killed in battle, it was almost impossible for their widows and orphans, or unmarried sisters or nieces, to survive without their male protector. In this context, the revelations in the Quran regarding marriage, like other Quranic revelations and reforms regarding inheritance, divorce, serving as a witness, etc., tended to improve women's position.

The Quran permits a man to marry up to four wives, provided that he is able to support and treat them equally: "Give orphans their property, and do not exchange the corrupt for the good; and devour not their property with your property; surely that is a great crime. If you are afraid you will not be able to deal justly with the orphans, marry women of your choice, two or three or four; but if you will not be able to deal justly [with them] only one" (4:3). This Quranic command restricts a male's right to an unlimited number of wives, while also using the umbrella of marriage as a protection for women in a violent society. As Quran 24:32 says, "Marry the spouseless among you, and your slaves and handmaidens that are righteous; if they are poor God will enrich them of his bounty; God is All-Embracing, All-Knowing."

Another verse, "You are never able to be fair and just between women even if that is your ardent desire" (4:129), has
been used in modern times by reformers to reject the possibil-
ity of equal justice among wives and to argue that the Quran
really preaches that monogamy is the ideal, as monogamy is
stressed in the later chapters of Quranic revelation. More conservative Muslims reject this interpretation as un-Islamic and
say that it reflects the tendency of reformers to imitate the West.

### Can Muslims marry non-Muslims?

Marriage regulations in Islam revolve around concerns regarding the faith of the children who will result from the union.
Marriage between a Muslim man and someone from a community not possessing a revelation is considered unlawful.
While it is preferable for Muslim men to marry Muslim
women, they are allowed to marry Christian or Jewish women,
because these women are "People of the Book," those who
have a divine revelation. Compatibility of belief is understood
to be critical to a harmonious marriage and family life. Whatever the male's official role as head of the household, women
tend to spend the most time with the children, particularly
when they are small, so children are more likely to be exposed to their mother's religion from an early age. Men therefore must select a wife who upholds monotheism and divine
revelation.

Muslim women must marry a Muslim or someone who converts to Islam. Under Islamic law, the male is recognized as the
head of the household, and in marriage his wife is expected to
take the nationality and status given by her husband's law.
The man is also responsible for the religious instruction of his
older children and for serving as their guardian, particularly

in matters of marriage. Thus the marriage of a Muslim woman to a non-Muslim man would represent the potential "loss" of the children from that union to Islam.

## What does Islam have to say about domestic violence?

Globally, domestic violence is a serious social problem, and the Muslim world is no exception. Many grassroots movements and women's organizations are working to eradicate it through education for both men and women about what the Quran teaches about marital relations.

In some Muslim societies, men use the Quran to justify domestic violence. However, many verses in the Quran teach that men and women are to be kind to and supportive of each other. Love and justice in family relationships are emphasized and cruelty is forbidden. Quran 30:21 states, "And among His signs is this, that He created for you mates from among yourselves, that you may dwell in tranquillity with them, and He has put love and mercy between your [hearts]: behold, verily in that are signs for those who reflect." Quran 4:19 further commands, "O you who believe! You are forbidden to inherit women against their will. Nor should you treat them with harshness. On the contrary live with them on a footing of kindness and equity. If you take a dislike to them it may be that you dislike a thing through which God brings about a great deal of good."

Chronologically, the last Quranic verse to be revealed that addressed relations between husband and wife was 9:71, in which women and men are described as being each other's protecting friends and guardians, emphasizing their cooperation in living together as partners, rather than adversaries or superiors and subordinates. Likewise, the *hadith* note Muhammad's respect for and protection of women. Muhammad said, "The best of you is he who is best to his wife." Muhammad's wife Aisha narrated that Muhammad never hit any servant or woman and never physically struck anyone with his own hand. Neither the Quran nor the hadith record Muhammad as ever mistreating or losing his temper with any of his wives, even when he was unhappy or dissatisfied.

Those who use the Quran to justify wife-beating point to 4:34, which says, "Good women are obedient, guarding in secret that which God has guarded. As for those from whom you fear disobedience, admonish them, then banish them to beds apart and strike them. But if they obey you, do not seek a way against them." In recent years scholars have argued that "obedience" refers to the woman's attitude toward God, not toward her husband. Furthermore, obedience in this verse is tied to the woman's guarding of her chastity, so that an obedient woman is one who does not commit sexual immorality. The word that is typically translated as "disobedience" (*nushuz*) refers to a disruption of marital harmony in which one spouse fails to fulfill the required duties of marriage. It is applied elsewhere in the Quran to both men and women. The end of the verse admonishes men not to mistreat women who obey them. Rather than granting men the right to strike their wives, reformers argue, this verse reminds men of their responsibility to treat women fairly.

Quran 4:34 lists three methods to be used in resolving marital disputes. First comes admonition or discussion between the husband and wife alone or with the assistance of arbiters. This practice, also recommended by 4:35 and 4:128, is also to be used for couples considering divorce. If this fails, the second option is physical separation, sleeping in separate beds, to give the couple space for cooling off and thinking about the future of the marital relationship. The third and final method is striking. This striking takes the singular form grammatically, so that only a single strike is permissible. Quran 4:34 was revealed early in the Medinan period of Muhammad's ministry, a time and place in which cruelty and violence against women remained rampant. Thus some Muslim scholars today argue that the single strike permitted in this verse was intended as a restriction on an existing practice, not as a recommended method for dealing with one's wife.

In the major hadith collections—Muslim, Bukhari, Tirmidhi, Abu Daud, Nasai, and Ibn Majah—hadith about striking all emphasize that striking should be done in such a way as not to cause pain or harm. These sources stress that, in cases where a single strike is used, it should be merely symbolic. The founder of the Shafii law school maintained that it is preferable to avoid striking altogether. Despite the fact that domestic violence continued to exist in male-dominated cultures and to be legitimated in the name of religion, neither the majority of Quranic verses nor the hadith support or permit it.

## How does Islam treat divorce?

In contrast to Catholicism, in Islam marriage is a contract, not a sacrament. Islam has always recognized the right to divorce under certain circumstances. In pre-Islamic times, Arab custom enabled a man to divorce at any time and for any reason, while his wife had no rights at all. However, the Quran established new guidelines to control a husband's arbitrary actions. It considers divorce, among the permitted things, to be a last resort and encourages arbitration between the spouses: "If you fear a split between a man and his wife, send for an arbiter from his family and an arbiter from her family [thus putting the wife's interests on a equal footing with those of her husband]. If both want to be reconciled, God will arrange things between them" (4:35). The Quran admonishes husbands faced with the prospect of proceeding to divorce to "either retain them [their wives] honorably or release them honorably" (65:2).

The seriousness of the act of divorce is reflected in the requirement given in the Quran that in order to make his divorce irrevocable a husband must pronounce "I divorce you" not once but three times, once each successive month for a period of three months. This is to allow time for reconciliation between husband and wife or, if there is no reconciliation and the wife is found to be pregnant, to arrange child support for the unborn child: "When you divorce women, divorce them when they have reached their period. Count their periods . . . and fear God your Lord. Do not expel them from their houses. . . . Those are limits set by God" (65:1).

Despite Quranic guidelines, an abbreviated form of divorce, which allows a man to declare "I divorce you" three times at once, became commonplace. Although considered a sinful abuse, it is nevertheless legally valid. This kind of divorce is a powerful example of how male-dominated customs overcame religious requirements and affected divorce rights in various Muslim countries for many generations.

Muslim countries have instituted a variety of laws, using the Quran and the courts, to control divorce proceedings and improve women's rights. In many countries today, Muslim women can obtain a divorce on a variety of grounds from the courts. Muslims who live in America or Europe must abide by civil law in obtaining a divorce. However, there are also many patriarchal societies where custom continues to allow extensive rights for men and more restricted rights of divorce for women. This illustrates the fact that problems with women's rights originate not from Islam but from patriarchy, which is still a strong force in many societies.

## Why are Muslims reluctant to shake hands?

There are two reasons why some Muslims are reluctant to shake hands when greeting another person. Conservatives believe that unrelated men and women should avoid touching each other due to the sexual overtones potentially associated with touching.

Some Muslims, like orthodox Jews, are reluctant to shake hands due to concerns about ritual purity. Traditional Shiis believe that non-Muslims are spiritually impure, so that physical contact with a non-Muslim, whether male or female, places the Muslim in a state of ritual impurity. Some Sunni Muslims also believe that non-Muslims are ritually impure, but Sunnis do not require ritual purification after coming into physical contact with non-Muslims.

## How do Muslims feel about pets, or petting animals?

There is no Quranic prohibition or condemnation of pets. Many *hadith* (Prophetic traditions) emphasize treating animals kindly and not overworking or beating them. One records the story of a woman who starved a cat to death and thus went to hell, while another describes a man who saved the life of a thirsty dog and thus went to heaven.

Dogs in the Islamic world are typically not allowed inside the house because they are considered to be unclean. Many Muslims believe that if anyone comes into contact with a dog's saliva, that person must repeat the ritual ablutions prior to prayer. A frequently cited hadith records that Muhammad forbade dogs inside the house for reasons of hygiene, but another hadith reports that the Prophet had a dog that used to play around him as he prayed outside his home. Cats, known for their cleanliness, lived in the household of Muhammad. He and some of his Companions were well known for their kindness to cats.

Some Muslims today argue that issues of disease that rendered dogs unhygienic in the past have largely been resolved through advances in veterinary medicine, so that contact with dogs is no longer a problem. Increasingly, Muslims, particularly those who were born in the United States and Europe, have dogs as pets. Others, however, believe that the prohibition of dogs inside the house recorded in the hadith remains applicable to every time and place.

## What is Islam's attitude toward alcohol and pork?

Both alcohol and pork are forbidden in Islam. Islamic law strictly prohibits the consumption, sale, and purchase of alcohol by Muslims, although in rare cases its use is permitted for medicinal purposes. The prohibition of the consumption of alcohol is based upon Quran 5:90-91, which states, "O you who believe! Intoxicants and gambling, dedication of stones, and divination by arrows are an abomination, among the works of Satan. Abstain from such work so that you may prosper. Satan's plan is to stir up enmity and hatred between you, with intoxicants and gambling, and hinder you from the remembrance of God, and from prayer. Will you not then abstain?" The specific intoxicant mentioned in this passage is date wine. Although a few jurists have argued that, according to a literal interpretation, only date wine is therefore forbidden, the overwhelming majority have interpreted this passage as a broad prohibition against any substance that produces an altered state of mind, including alcohol and narcotics.

Many countries that have implemented the Shariah (Islamic law) have banned alcohol, usually for Muslims and non-Muslims alike. Examples include Iran, Pakistan, Sudan, Saudi Arabia, Libya, and portions of Malaysia. Some countries with secular regimes, such as Turkey and Egypt, have instituted strict laws prohibiting narcotics but have allowed controlled importation, sale, and consumption of alcoholic beverages. Islamist organizations typically support a complete ban on alcohol.

In the United States and Europe, recent Muslim immigrants have made abstention from consumption of and contact with alcoholic beverages a visible and defining characteristic of their identity as Muslims. The Black Muslim movement particularly supports an absolute ban on liquor, as do many African-American Muslims. This stands in marked contrast to earlier generations of Muslim immigrants who, although often abstaining from alcohol themselves, have nevertheless owned, operated, and worked in establishments that sell alcohol, including bars. Muslim communities living in the West today debate and differ about whether Muslims should work in places that sell, consume, or produce alcohol, including vineyards, restaurants, and grocery stores. A similar concern for some is whether it is permissible for a Muslim to accept an invitation to dinner knowing that alcohol may or will be served as part of the meal, whether at a restaurant or in the privacy of someone's home.

The dietary prohibition against pork also comes from the Quran. Quran 5:3 states, "You are forbidden to eat carrion, blood, and the flesh of swine, as well as whatever is slaughtered in the name of any one other than God." Quran 6:145 confirms this prohibition. Some Muslims further believe that, because the pig is an animal known to carry germs and diseases, particularly trichinosis, the consumption of pork products is unhealthy and unhygienic, in addition to being prohibited by the Quran. Physical contact with pork or pork products is believed to render a person or object impure, although this impurity can be removed by either washing or removing the offending substance.

American Muslims generally respect the prohibition of pork and pork products. Just as with alcohol, some Muslims are reluctant to accept dinner invitations to non-Muslim homes for fear of unknowingly being served a pork product. The widespread use of pork products and by-products by American food manufacturers creates difficulties for American Muslims seeking to avoid pork. Pork lard is commonly used in the United States as shortening, so it may be concealed in seemingly harmless food items like cookies, and potato chips may be fried in it. Some American Muslims read every label carefully to verify that no pork products have been used; others believe that such detailed attention is unnecessary. This raises the further question of the permissibility of eating in restaurants, particularly fast-food restaurants that fry their foods, because the consumer does not know what oils and fats are used for frying and other cooking. Some mosques and Islamic centers circulate lists of specific products known to contain either pork or alcohol (even mustard, because some mustards are made with white wine), so that their faith communities can avoid them.

## Why are Muslims against dancing?

Muslims have a variety of opinions about dancing, depending on their country of origin, how conservative their understanding of Islam is, the type of dancing in question, and where the dancing takes place. Dancing between unmarried couples is generally disapproved of, since dancing typically involves touching, an action considered inappropriate between unmarried people of opposite genders. In addition, many Muslims are concerned that permitting their children to attend American-style dances, such as those sponsored by junior and senior high schools, will lead to their dating non-Muslims or to sexual activity.

This does not mean that all dancing is forbidden in Islam. In many Middle Eastern countries, belly dancing and folk dancing have long been part of celebrations, particularly weddings. Especially popular are single-sex group dances that are performed in circular, cluster, or chain formations and consist of rhythmic stamping and stepping with the feet and clapping with the hands. Another style of dancing, particularly in tribal cultures, consists of a series of maneuvers with a weapon, such as a sword, dagger, spear, or stick.

In addition, some Sufi orders, such as the Mawlawi/Mevlevi order, also known as the "Whirling Dervishes," use dance as a devotional tool in their quest for a direct spiritual experience of God and in imitation of the order of the universe. Islamic forms of dance tend to follow the broader Islamic artistic pattern of symmetry, geometry, and rhythm. Dance in Islamic culture has therefore tended to feature a series of individual units arranged to form a larger design, all of which are symmetrical and follow an arabesque pattern (an infinite series of circles or other shapes). This pattern is a symbolic representation of belief in the oneness of God (*tawhid*).

## Why are some Muslims opposed to music?

Muslims sometimes oppose rock music because of the culture that generally tends to accompany it rather than the musical form in itself. Many young Muslims raised in the West listen to rock music because it is such a pervasive part of American youth culture.

Some Muslim parents, like many non-Muslims, object to much Western music, particularly rock music and hip-hop, because of the emphasis of the lyrics on sex, drugs, alcohol consumption, and violence. They are also concerned about allowing young people to attend rock concerts, because sex, drugs, and alcohol tend to be present.

Like the Christian rock movement, some Muslims have responded to these concerns by forming their own rock and even rap bands with lyrics that are religiously inspired. The songs of a Washington, D.C.–based group, Native Deen (*deen* is Arabic for religion), combine traditional Islamic messages— praying regularly, avoiding sex and violence, fasting during Ramadan, and generally struggling to be a good Muslim— with a hip-hop beat. The folk singer Yusuf Islam (the former Cat Stevens) has composed "Muslim" pop music for both adults and children, such as his best-selling song "A Is for Allah." He has also put his musical talents to use in ways reminiscent of the Farm Aid concerts and the *Feed the World* album of the 1980s by hosting fund-raising concerts for Muslim causes throughout the world, including earthquake relief in Turkey and assistance to the Muslims of Bosnia.

Some ultraconservative Muslims, such as the Taliban of Afghanistan, believe that music should not be a part of Muslim life at all because they consider music to be intoxicating. In medieval times, as now, strict scholars objected to the kind of lifestyle represented by professional singers and the places where people gathered to listen to popular music. However, historically music has been an important art form throughout the Muslim world. The most important musical form in Islam is Quran recitation, an art form in which annual competitions are held. Recordings of Quran recitation are sold throughout the Muslim world, and some of Islam's most famous singers have been Quran reciters or singers who have imitated Quran recitation in their music, such as the Egyptian singer Umm Kulthum. Likewise, the Muslim call to prayer (*adhan*) is sung or chanted, rather than strictly spoken. Music has played an important role in religious festivals and life cycle events such as birth, marriage, and circumcision.

The Sufi orders typically use music as part of their devotions, both vocally, through repetition of words or phrases and in chanting, and instrumentally. Music is a vehicle for spiritual transcendence and a means of attaining the experience of divine ecstasy.

Folk music has also been an important expression of culture throughout the Muslim world, often as a venue for heroic and love-related poetry, as well as moral and devotional themes. The music produced by the Muslims of Andalusia, like their poetry, had an enormous impact on the development of classical music in Europe. Some modern musicians, such as Cheb Mami, the "father" of Algerian *rai* music who sang "Desert Rose" with the British rock star Sting, have incorporated Western instruments, particularly electronics, and techniques into their folk traditions.

## *How do Muslims greet each other and why?*

Muslims greet each other with the Arabic phrase *As-salaam alaykum*, "Peace be upon you," to which the appropriate response is *Wa-alaykum as-salaam*, "And peace be upon you also." The Quran commands Muslims to greet each other in this way as a reflection of the peaceful relationships that are intended to exist between Muslims, based upon their common faith and submission to the will of God.

Quran 10:10 records that Muslims who enter heaven will greet each other in this way: "Their cry there will be, 'Glory to you, O God!' and 'Peace!' will be their greeting therein!" Quran 14:23 also records, "But those who believe and work righteousness will be admitted to Gardens beneath which rivers flow—to dwell there forever with their Lord's permission. Their greeting therein will be: 'Peace!'"

## *Why do Muslims say "Peace be upon him?" What does PBUH mean?*

PBUH stands for "Peace Be Upon Him." Muslims repeat this every time they refer to Muhammad or any of the prophets (Jesus, Moses, etc.). Some Muslims use the longer phrase "God's Blessings and Peace Be Upon Him," which is the English equivalent of the full Arabic phrase *Salah Allah Alayhi wa-Salaam.* This is abbreviated as SAAS. These abbreviations are used in written documents throughout the Muslim world, both privately and publicly, including in government documents in some countries.

The use of PBUH or the repetition of the phrase "Peace be upon him" in speech reflects the belief that Muslims should at all times remember the special role of the Prophet and request God's blessings upon him in order to obtain blessings for themselves. The Quran commands this remembrance. Quran 33:56 states, "God and His angels send blessings on the Prophet. O you who believe! Send blessings on him, and salute him with all respect."

This phrase also reflects the important role Muhammad plays in Islam as the living embodiment of the revelation contained in the Quran. It is through Muhammad's life, love for God and for humanity, and vision of how human beings should live in this world that Muslims believe they can know the will of God.

# VIOLENCE AND TERRORISM

## What is jihad?

Jihad (to strive or struggle) is sometimes referred to as the Sixth Pillar of Islam. The importance of jihad is rooted in the Quran's command to struggle (the literal meaning of the word *jihad*) in the path of God and in the example of the Prophet Muhammad and his early Companions.

The history of the Muslim community from Muhammad to the present can be read within the framework of what the Quran teaches about jihad. These Quranic teachings have been of essential significance to Muslim self-understanding, piety, mobilization, expansion, and defense. Jihad as struggle pertains to the difficulty and complexity of living a good life: struggling against the evil in oneself—to be virtuous and moral, making a serious effort to do good works and help to reform society. Depending on the circumstances in which one lives, it also can mean fighting injustice and oppression, spreading and defending Islam, and creating a just society through preaching, teaching, and, if necessary, armed struggle or holy war.

The two broad meanings of jihad, nonviolent and violent, are contrasted in a well-known Prophetic tradition. It is said that when Muhammad returned from battle he told his followers, "We return from the lesser jihad [warfare] to the greater jihad." The greater jihad is the more difficult and more important struggle against one's ego, selfishness, greed, and evil.

117

In its most general meaning, jihad refers to the obligation incumbent on all Muslims, individuals and the community, to follow and realize God's will: to lead a virtuous life and to extend the Islamic community through preaching, education, example, writing, etc. Jihad also includes the right, indeed the obligation, to defend Islam and the community from aggression. Throughout history, the call to jihad has rallied Muslims to the defense of Islam. The Afghan *mujahidin* recently fought a decade-long jihad against Soviet occupation.

Jihad is a concept with multiple meanings, used and abused throughout Islamic history. Although jihad has always been an important part of the Islamic tradition, in recent years some have maintained that it is a universal religious obligation for all true Muslims to join the jihad to promote Islamic reform or revolution. Some look around them and see a world dominated by corrupt authoritarian regimes and a wealthy elite minority concerned solely with its own economic prosperity and awash in Western culture and values. Western governments are perceived as propping up oppressive regimes and exploiting the region's human and natural resources, robbing Muslims of their culture and their option to be governed according to their own choice and to live in a more just society.

Mainstream Islamic activists believe that the restoration of Muslim power and prosperity requires a return to Islam, a political or social revolution to create more Islamically oriented states or societies. A radicalized violent minority combine militancy with messianic visions to inspire and mobilize an army of God whose jihad they believe will liberate Muslims at home and abroad. Despite the fact that jihad is not supposed to be used for aggressive warfare, it has been and continues to be so used by some rulers, governments, and individuals such as Saddam Hussein in the Gulf War of 1991, the Taliban in Afghanistan, and Osama bin Laden and al-Qaeda.

## *Does the Quran condone terrorism?*

This is the kind of question no one asks of his or her own religion; we save it for others! Historically, some Muslims have engaged in terrorism and used religion to justify their actions. For many who have little previous knowledge of Islam or Muslims, acts of terrorism committed by extremists, in particular 9/11, raise the question of whether there is something in Islam or the Quran that fosters violence and terrorism.

Islam, like all world religions, neither supports nor requires illegitimate violence. The Quran does not advocate or condone terrorism. The God of the Quran is consistently portrayed as a God of mercy and compassion as well as a just judge. Every chapter of the Quran begins with a reference to God's mercy and compassion; throughout the Quran in many contexts, Muslims are reminded to be merciful and just. Indeed, whenever a pious Muslim begins an activity such as a meal, writing a letter, or driving a car, he or she says, "Al-Rahman al-Rahim" (In the name of God the Merciful and Compassionate). However, Islam does permit, indeed at times requires, Muslims to defend themselves and their families, religion, and community from aggression.

Like all scriptures, Islamic sacred texts must be read within the social and political contexts in which they were revealed. It is not surprising that the Quran, like the Hebrew scriptures or Old Testament, has verses that address fighting and the conduct of war. The world in which the Islamic community emerged was a rough neighborhood. Arabia and the city of Mecca, in which Muhammad lived and received God's revelation, were beset by tribal raids and cycles of vengeance and vendetta. The broader Near East, in which Arabia was located, was itself divided between two warring superpowers, the Byzantine (Eastern Roman) and the Sasanian (Persian) empires.

The earliest Quranic verses dealing with the right to engage in a "defensive" jihad, or struggle, were revealed shortly after the *hijra* (emigration) of Muhammad and his followers to Medina in flight from their persecution in Mecca. At a time when they were forced to fight for their lives, Muhammad is told: "Leave is given to those who fight because they were wronged—surely God is able to help them—who were expelled from their homes wrongfully for saying, 'Our Lord is God'" (22:39–40). The defensive nature of jihad is clearly emphasized in 2:190, "And fight in the way of God with those who fight you, but aggress not: God loves not the aggressors." At critical points throughout the years, Muhammad received revelations from God that provided guidelines for the jihad.

As the Muslim community grew, questions quickly emerged as to what was proper behavior during times of war. The Quran provided detailed guidelines and regulations regarding the conduct of war: who is to fight and who is exempted (48:17, 9:91), when hostilities must cease (2:192), and how prisoners should be treated (47:4). Most important, verses such as 2:294 emphasized that warfare and the response to violence and aggression must be proportional: "Whoever transgresses against you, respond in kind."

However, Quranic verses also underscore that peace, not violence and warfare, is the norm. Permission to fight the enemy is balanced by a strong mandate for making peace: "If your enemy inclines toward peace, then you too should seek peace and put your trust in God" (8:61) and "Had Allah wished, He would have made them dominate you, and so if they leave you alone and do not fight you and offer you peace, then Allah allows you no way against them" (4:90). From the earliest times, it was forbidden in Islam to kill noncombatants as well as women and children and monks and rabbis, who were given the promise of immunity unless they took part in the fighting.

But what of those verses, sometimes referred to as the "sword verses," that call for killing unbelievers, such as, "When the sacred months have passed, slay the idolaters wherever you find them, and take them, and confine them, and lie in wait for them at every place of ambush" (9:5)? This is one of a number of Quranic verses that are cited by critics to demonstrate the inherently violent nature of Islam and its scripture. These same verses have also been selectively used (or abused) by religious extremists to develop a theology of hate and intolerance and to legitimate unconditional warfare against unbelievers.

During the period of expansion and conquest, many of the *ulama* (religious scholars) enjoyed royal patronage and provided a rationale for caliphs to pursue their imperial dreams and extend the boundaries of their empires. They said that the "sword verses" abrogated or overrode the earlier Quranic verses that limited jihad to defensive war: in fact, however, the full intent of "When the sacred months have passed, slay the idolaters wherever you find them" is missed or distorted when quoted in isolation. For it is followed and qualified by: "But if they repent and fulfill their devotional obligations and pay the zakat [the charitable tax on Muslims], then let them go their way, for God is forgiving and kind"(9:5). The same is true of another often quoted verse: "Fight those who believe not in God nor the Last Day, nor hold that forbidden which hath been forbidden by God and His Apostle, nor hold the religion of truth [even if they are] of the People of the Book," which is often cited without the line that follows, "Until they pay the tax with willing submission, and feel themselves subdued" (9:29).

Throughout history, the sacred scriptures of Judaism, Christianity, and Islam have been used and abused, interpreted and misinterpreted, to justify resistance and liberation struggles, extremism and terrorism, holy and unholy wars. Terrorists like Osama bin Laden and others go beyond classical Islam's criteria for a just jihad and recognize no limits but their own, employing any weapons or means. They reject Islamic law's regulations regarding the goals and legitimate means for a valid jihad: that violence must be proportional and that only the necessary amount of force should be used to repel the enemy, that innocent civilians should not be targeted, and that jihad must be declared by the ruler or head of state. Today, individuals and groups, religious and lay, seize the right to declare and legitimate unholy wars of terrorism in the name of Islam.

## How can Islam be used to justify terrorism, hijackings, and hostage taking?

While the atrocities and acts of terrorism committed by violent extremists have connected Islam with terrorism, the Islamic tradition places limits on the use of violence and rejects terrorism, hijackings, and hostage taking. As with other faiths, mainstream and normative doctrines and laws are ignored, distorted, or hijacked and misinterpreted by a radical fringe. Islamic law, drawing on the Quran, sets out clear guidelines for the conduct of war and rejects acts of terrorism. Among other things, it is quite specific in calling for the protection of noncombatants as well as for proportional retaliation.

As the Muslim community grew, questions quickly emerged about who had religious and political authority, how to handle rebellion and civil war, what was proper behavior during times of war and peace, and how to rationalize and legitimate expansion and conquest, violence and resistance. Answers were developed by referring to Quranic injunctions and the practice of Muhammad and his companions.

The Quran provides detailed guidelines and regulations regarding war: who should fight (48:17, 9:91), when fighting should end (2:192), how to treat prisoners (47:4). It emphasizes proportionality in warfare: "Whoever transgresses against you, respond in kind"(2:194). Other verses provide a strong mandate for making peace: "If your enemy inclines toward peace, then you too should seek peace and put your trust in God" (8:61) and "Had Allah wished, He would have made them dominate you, and so if they leave you alone and do not fight you and offer you peace, then Allah allows you no way against them" (4:90).

From its origins, the Islamic community faced rebellion and civil wars, violence and terrorism, epitomized by groups like the Kharijites and Assassins. The Kharijites were a pious but puritanical and militant extremist group that broke with the caliph Ali and later assassinated him. The Assassins lived apart in secret communities from which they were guided by a series of Grand Masters, who ruled from the mountain fortress of Alamut in northern Persia. The Assassins' jihad against the Seljuq Dynasty terrorized princes, generals, and *ulama* (scholars), whom they murdered in the name of the Hidden Imam. They struck such terror in the hearts of their Muslim and Crusader enemies that their exploits in Persia and Syria earned them a name and memory in history long after they were overrun and the Mongols executed their last Grand Master in 1256.

The response of Sunni Islam and Islamic law was to marginalize extremists and develop a political theory that emphasized stability over chaos and anarchy. This, of course, did not dissuade all from the extremist path. In more recent decades, alongside mainstream Islamic political opposition, terrorist groups have risen up to challenge regimes and terrorize their populations and attack foreign interests. Often they portray themselves as the "true believers" struggling against repressive regimes and in the midst of a "pagan" society of unbelief. They attempt to impose their ideological brand of Islam and "hijack" Islamic doctrines such as jihad, claiming to be defending true Islam, to legitimate their illegitimate use of violence and acts of terrorism.

In Egypt, groups like Egypt's Islamic Jihad and other extremist groups assassinated President Anwar Sadat and other government officials, slaughtered tourists in Luxor, burned churches, and killed Christians. In Algeria, the Armed Islamic Group has engaged in a campaign of terror against the Algerian government. Osama bin Laden and al-Qaeda undertook a global war of terror against Muslim governments and America, distorting Islam and countering Islamic law in issuing their own *fatwas* (legal opinions) in an attempt to legitimate their war and call for attacks against civilians (noncombatants). Although these groups tend to receive the most media coverage because of the high-profile atrocities they commit, they represent only an extremist minority, not the majority of Muslims.

## Does Islam permit suicide bombers?

On February 25, 1994, Dr. Baruch Goldstein, a Jewish settler who had emigrated to Israel from the United States, walked into the Mosque of the Patriarch in Hebron and opened fire, killing twenty-nine Muslim worshipers during their Friday congregational prayer. In response, Hamas (Islamic Resistance Movement) introduced a new type of warfare in the Palestinian-Israeli conflict, suicide bombing. Promising swift revenge for the Hebron massacre, the Hamas militia, the Qassem Brigade, undertook operations within Israel itself, in Galilee, Jerusalem, and Tel Aviv. In Israel-Palestine, the use of suicide bombing increased exponentially during the second (al-Aqsa) *intifada* (uprising), which began in September 2000. The most horrific example of suicide bombings or attacks was seen in the 9/11 attacks against the World Trade Center and the Pentagon.

Traditionally, Muslims are unconditionally forbidden to commit suicide, because only God has the right to take the life he has granted. There is only one phrase in the Quran that appears relevant to suicide: "O you who believe! Do not consume your wealth in the wrong way—rather only through trade mutually agreed to, and do not kill yourselves. Surely God is Merciful toward you" (4:29). However, many Muslim exegetes have believed that "do not kill yourselves" can mean "do not kill each other" since it fits the context of the verse. The subject of suicide is therefore little discussed in exegetical literature. The Prophetic traditions (*hadith*), however, frequently, clearly, and absolutely prohibit suicide. Punishment for self-slaughter consists of the unending repetition of the act by which the suicide was committed. Many commentators, however, have been reluctant to say that a person who commits suicide is condemned eternally to hell.

Historically both Sunni and Shii Muslims have generally forbidden "sacrificial religious suicide" and acts of terrorism. The Nizari Ismailis, popularly called the Assassins, who in the eleventh and twelfth centuries were notorious for sending suicidal assassins against their enemies, were rejected by mainstream Islam as fanatics. However, in the late twentieth century, the issue resurfaced as many, Shii and Sunni alike, came to equate suicide bombing with martyrdom, relinquishing one's life for the faith. Although usually associated with the Israeli-Palestinian conflict, in fact suicide bombings have also occurred in Lebanon, Indonesia, and elsewhere. In Lebanon, they were used by Hizbollah and al-Jihad in attacks such as those against the U.S. Marine barracks and French military headquarters in Beirut in 1983, in which several hundred were killed.

In Israel-Palestine, increased Israeli violence, brutality, and targeted assassinations reinforced the belief among many Palestinians and Muslims that so-called suicide bombers were committing not an act of suicide but one of self-sacrifice, engaged in resistance and retaliation against Israeli occupation and oppression. As student posters at universities in the West Bank and Gaza declared: "Israel has nuclear bombs, we have human bombs." Or as a Palestinian fighter remarked: "The Israelis blow us up. Why shouldn't I go to Israel and take some of them with me?"

The use of religious concepts like jihad and martyrdom to justify and legitimate suicide bombing provides a powerful incentive: the prospect of being a glorified hero in this life and enjoying Paradise in the next. Suicide bombings, especially those that target innocent civilians or noncombatants, have precipitated a sharp debate in the Muslim world, garnering both support and condemnation on religious grounds. Prominent religious leaders have differed sharply in their legal opinions (*fatwas*). Sheikh Ahmad Yasin, the religious leader and founder of Hamas, and Akram Sabri, the Mufti of Jerusalem, as well as many other Arab and Palestinian religious leaders, have argued that suicide bombing is necessary and justified. However, others condemn suicide bombings, in particular those that target civilians, as terrorism.

Prominent Islamic scholars and leaders have been sharply divided in opinion. Sheikh al-Sheikh, the head of Egypt's venerable al-Azhar Mosque and former Grand Mufti of Saudi Arabia, has condemned all suicide bombing as un-Islamic and forbidden by Islam. Sheikh Muhammad Sayad Tantawi, the Grand Mufti of Egypt and a leading religious authority, has drawn a sharp distinction between suicide bombings that are acts of self-sacrifice and self-defense and the killing of non-combatants, women, and children, which he has consistently condemned. Sheikh Yusuf al-Qardawi, among the most influential religious authorities, has given fatwas that recognize suicide bombing as an act of self-defense, the giving of one's life for God with the hope that God will grant him or her Paradise. Like others, Qardawi has legitimated the killing of civilians, arguing that Israel is a militant and military society in which both men and women serve in the military and reserves and that if an elderly person or a child is killed in such acts, it is an involuntary killing.

A key issue that has emerged in these debates is that of proportionality, that the response or retaliation must be in proportion to the crime committed. Those who seek to justify the killing of civilians argue that in Israel there are no innocent civilians both because Israeli society is a military society and because the Israeli occupation and settlements indiscriminately threaten Palestinian civilians.

## Why are Muslims so violent?

The acts of Muslim extremists in recent years, from hostage taking and kidnappings to the World Trade Center and Pentagon attacks of 9/11, lead many to ask why Islam and Muslims are so violent. Islam, from the Quran to Islamic law, does not permit terrorism and places limits on the use of violence. It does permit, and in some circumstances even requires, the use of force in self-defense or the defense of Islam and the Islamic community. However, there is often a fine line between legitimate and illegitimate use of force, defensive and offensive battle and warfare, resistance and terrorism. While religion can be a powerful force for good, historically it has also been used to legitimate violence and warfare. The three great monotheistic traditions from biblical times to the present represent long histories of the positive and negative power of religion, its ability to create and to destroy.

Muslim rulers and governments past and present have used religion to legitimate and mobilize support for political expansion and imperialism. Religious extremists from early groups such as the Kharijites to contemporary movements like Egypt's Islamic Jihad and al-Qaeda have employed a radical theological vision, based upon distorted interpretations of scripture and doctrine, to justify violence and terrorism against their own societies and the international community. They have created a world in which those who do not accept and follow their beliefs, Muslim and non-Muslim alike, are the enemy to be fought and exterminated by any means.

The issue of violence in Muslim societies is further compounded by the violent character of many states. Authoritarian rulers and governments, secular and religious, use force, violence, repression, and terror to assure their stability and security at home and, in some instances, to expand their influence abroad. Failed economies, high unemployment, shortages of housing, a growing gap between rich and poor, and widespread corruption exacerbate the situation, contributing to the growth of radicalism and extremist opposition. The extent to which outside powers, including America and Europe, are seen as supporting oppressive regimes or "colonizing" and exploiting Muslim societies contributes to the appeal of violence and terrorism. These conditions and grievances create a seedbed from which the Saddam Husseins and Osama bin Ladens of the world find ready recruits in their unholy wars.

## *Do Muslims support extremist and terrorist groups?*

Islam and Islamic law have consistently condemned terrorism (the killing of noncombatants). Like the members of all religious faiths, Muslims have had to deal with religious extremism and terrorism from their earliest days. The response of the mainstream majority to groups like the Kharijites and the Assassins and more contemporary groups like Islamic Jihad in Egypt or al-Qaeda has been to condemn, combat, and marginalize them.

However, it is often rather difficult to distinguish between the legitimate and illegitimate use of violence, and between protest, resistance, and liberation movements and terrorist organizations. For Shii Muslims, Hussein's seventh-century battle against the caliph Yazid (the son of the general who had challenged the right of Hussein's father, Ali, to rule as fourth caliph and after Ali's death seized power and created the Umayyad Empire) was a legitimate struggle against those who had usurped power that rightfully belonged to the anointed leaders (Imams) of the Islamic community, descendants of Ali and Muhammad. Subsequent Shii guerrilla or revolutionary movements against Sunni rulers during the Umayyad and Abbasid caliphates were seen as part of the ongoing attempt to overthrow illegitimate rulers.

In more recent times, the acts of Osama bin Laden and al-Qaeda and similar extremist organizations that have terrorized Muslim and non-Muslim societies present a clear example of terrorism. But many others do not. The line between the legitimate and illegitimate use of force, between moderates and extremists, between populist movements and terrorists, is often a subject of dispute. The difference between aggression and self-defense, between resistance and terrorism, often depends on where one stands. Christians and Jews regard their traditions as committed to peace and social justice and their societies as engaging only in wars of self-defense but are often quick to believe that other traditions and peoples (such as Islam and Muslims) are more militant and warlike. Our wars are defensive, not offensive, "just wars"; "their" wars are unholy wars.

The distinction between movements of national liberation and terrorist organizations is often dependent upon one's religious or political vantage point. America's revolutionary heroes were rebels and terrorists for the British crown, as were Israel's Menachem Begin and Yitzak Shamir, of the Irgun and Stern gangs respectively. South Africa's Nelson Mandela of the African National Congress was once regarded by the United States as a terrorist leading a terrorist movement. Yesterday's terrorists may be just that—terrorists—or they may become the statesmen of today.

Determining who qualifies as a terrorist continues to be difficult. For years, the American government refused to yield to repeated British requests that it rein in Irish-American involvement with and support for the Irish Republican Army, which the British government labeled a terrorist organization. However, the United States did accede to similar requests from Israeli and American Jewish organizations for measures to prevent similar support for "radical Islamic fundamentalist" organizations such as Hamas. Christian liberation theology and its derivative movements in Latin and Central America have been alternatively described as crypto-Marxist revolutionary forces and as authentic populist religious movements. Often the answer to the questions "What is extremism?" and "What is terrorism?" has depended upon where one stands.

## Do most Muslim organizations support terrorism?

From early Islamic centuries to the present, Muslims have created many religious, educational, political, and social welfare institutions and organizations. Among them are hospitals, universities, schools, clinics, day care centers, student hostels and camps, refugee relief agencies, legal aid societies, social services, banks, insurance companies, publishing houses, and professional associations of physicians, lawyers, journalists, and scientists. Many have been charitable organizations supported by religious endowments (*waqf*, pl. *awqaf*) of land or money designated specifically for charitable purposes or by the financial support of governments or wealthy individuals.

In recent years, governments with oil wealth such as Libya, Saudi Arabia, and the United Arab Emirates have created organizations to support missionary activities, the preaching and spread of Islam globally through the building of mosques, Islamic centers, schools and libraries, and the translation and distribution of the Quran and other religious texts.

The majority of organizations and societies have been part of mainstream society, often providing affordable educational, medical, legal, social services in countries where governments are unable or unwilling to do so. Islamically inspired organizations and societies have created networks that provide employment, housing, education, and financial support for the poor and victims of disasters such as earthquakes and for the families of those killed in battle. At the same time, religious extremists have also created their own networks of services. Charitable activities by both mainstream and extremist organizations and societies have often been supported not only domestically but also with funds from other parts of the Muslim world and from charitable organizations established in America and in Europe.

In recent years, governments have become concerned about support for terrorist organizations coming from charitable organizations. The problem has been compounded at times by the difficulty of distinguishing between resistance movements and extremists who commit acts of terrorism. For years Britain chided the United States for allowing Irish-Americans to provide support to the Irish Republican Army, which Britain condemned as a terrorist organization; while some claimed to support the IRA but not its military wing, others labeled this as disingenuous hair splitting. Support from Muslims (both individuals and organizations) for social welfare services or organizations connected with groups like Hizbollah in Lebanon and Hamas in Israel-Palestine gives rise to similar questions. Since the late 1990s, for example, antiterrorism legislation in the United States and Britain has identified as terrorist organizations groups like Hizbollah, Hamas, and others to whose charitable wings donations had previously been legal.

## *Do Muslims have a martyrdom complex?*

In Islam as in Christianity, martyrdom—a willingness to die for one's faith or in order to protect the religious community—has a long and special history and tradition. Martyrs who sacrifice their lives to establish Islamic ideals or to defend those ideals hold an important place in Islam.

To die for one's faith is the highest form of witness to God. The Arabic/Quranic word for martyr, *shahid,* means "witness," from the same root as the word for the Muslim profession of faith (*shahada*), which bears witness that "there is no God but God, and Muhammad is the messenger of God."

The Quran has many passages that support the notion of martyrdom and that comfort those left behind. For example:

If you are killed in the cause of God or you die, the forgive-
ness and mercy of God are better than all that you amass.
And if you die or are killed, even so it is to God that you
will return. (3:157–58)

Never think that those who are killed in the way of God
are dead. They are alive with their Lord, well provided for.
(3:169)

*Hadith* literature, stories about what Muhammad said and did,
also provides many affirmations of the rewards for those who
die for Islam. Muslim tradition teaches that martyrs are distinguished from others in the life after death in several ways.
Their self-sacrifice renders them free of sin, and therefore they
are not subject to the postmortem interrogation of the angels
Nakir and Munkar. They bypass "purgatory" and proceed to
one of the highest locations in heaven near the Throne of
God. As a result of their purity, they are buried in the clothes
in which they died and do not need to be washed before burial.

Both Sunni and Shii traditions value and esteem martyrdom in their beliefs and devotions. Sunni Islam has historically valorized martyrdom through veneration of the struggles
(*jihads*) of the early Medinan community with the Meccan Arabs. Throughout Islamic history the call to jihad in the path of
God served as a rallying cry. In the seventeenth and eighteenth
centuries, leaders of Islamic revivalist movements from Africa
and Arabia to Southeast Asia cast their struggles as jihads. Thus
those who died were guaranteed paradise as martyrs.

Shii Islam has a particularly powerful martyrdom tradition
and legacy, starting with the martyrdom of the Prophet's
grandson Hussein, who with his small "righteous" band of
followers was slaughtered by the army of the Sunni caliph

Yazid. This sacred tragedy became the paradigm for Shii theology and spirituality and is ritually reenacted annually in Shii communities. It has expressed itself in the special place given to visiting graves of the martyrs and mourning and emulating the suffering of Hussein and his companions with prayer, weeping, and self-flagellation—a ritual analogous to the commemoration of the passion and death of Jesus Christ.

Since the dawn of European colonialism, a new, broader understanding of martyrdom has developed. Soldiers killed in wars of independence against European colonial powers were often called martyrs. Since the late twentieth century, Muslims have used the term *jihad* for all struggles in defense of Muslim territory; thus those who die in such battles are martyrs. Martyrdom was a powerful theme in the Iran-Iraq war. Both Sunni Iraqis and Shii Iranians relied on the promise of martyrdom to motivate their soldiers. In postrevolutionary Iran, the tradition was reflected in the creation of martyr cemeteries for those who died in the Iran-Iraq war and for the revolution's clergy and supporters who were murdered or assassinated by opposition forces.

Martyrdom, like jihad, has become a global phenomenon, a common term of praise for those who have died in struggles (jihads) in Palestine (whether members of secular or Islamic Palestinian groups), Iran, Egypt, and Lebanon as well as Azerbaijan, Bosnia, Chechnya, Kashmir, and the southern Philippines.

## *Why do they hate us?*

Anti-Americanism (along with anti-Europeanism) is a broad-based phenomenon that cuts across Arab and Muslim societies. It is driven not only by the blind hatred or religious zealotry of extremists but also by frustration and anger with U.S. foreign policy among the mainstream in the Muslim world.

The West's espousal of self-determination, democratization, and human rights is often seen as a hypocritical "double standard" when compared to its policies, what it actually does— for instance, imposing sanctions against Pakistan for its development of a nuclear weapon while failing to press Israel and India on their nuclear development. The moral will so evident in America's helping Kosovo is seen by many Muslims as totally absent in the U.S. policy of permissive neglect in the Chechnyan and Kashmiri conflicts. On the other hand, America's stance on human rights has been undermined by the abuse of Muslim prisoners in Abu Gharib prison in Iraq and Guantanamo Bay, Cuba.

Another inflammatory issue involves the significant presence of U.S. military and arms in the Gulf, which critics perceive as a neocolonialist military influence. The American presence is equated with support for unpopular authoritarian regimes and pressure on Arab governments to comply with U.S. foreign policy objectives, especially with respect to Israel and Palestine. This long litany of grievances stretching over many years feeds the anger of many mainstream Arabs and Muslims, as well as extremists.

Globalization of communications has created a situation in which Arabs (Muslims and Christians) and Muslims around the world often see more than we see. Unlike the past, today international Arab and Muslim media are no longer solely dependent on Western reporters and channels. While America's overseas media presence (reporters and overseas posts) and coverage have waned over the past decade, television stations like al-Jazeera and others provide daily coverage of the violence in many Muslim countries. They show, for example, the violence and acts of terror committed by both sides as well as the disproportionate firepower used against Palestinians by Israelis armed with American-supplied weapons, F-16s, and

Apache helicopters. America's record of overwhelming support of Israel—witnessed in its levels of aid to Israel, the U.S. voting record in the United Nations, and official statements by the administration and State Department—has proved to be a powerful lightning rod for Muslim anger over injustice.

## Why was Salman Rushdie condemned to death?

In 1988, Salman Rushdie published *The Satanic Verses*, a novel that caused an uproar among Muslims throughout the world because of its perceived disrespect for Islam, the Prophet Muhammad, and the Quran. The title of the novel refers to a story about Muhammad (which many Muslims believe to be apocryphal) in which Satan interferes with the revelation Muhammad is receiving. As a consequence of this interference, Muhammad is said to have recited two verses saying that al-Lat, al-Uzza, and Manat, three goddesses who had been worshipped by the Quraysh (the people of Muhammad's tribe), could be intermediaries between God and man. Muhammad discovered that this message had come from Satan, and these "satanic verses" were eliminated. Muhammad then received a new revelation describing the three goddesses as figments of the imagination deserving no worship at all.

Although this story appears in the accounts of two early historians, it is not to be found in the Quran or in any of the official collections of traditions (*hadith*) compiled about Muhammad in the ninth century. Moreover, it is contradicted by other stories and by the Quran itself. In the past it had attracted more interest in the West than in the Islamic world. Rushdie's use of the title, with its suggestion of Muhammad's receiving a satanic revelation, coupled with what many regarded as blasphemous treatment of the Prophet and his wives, generated Muslim protests and demonstrations, first in England, where the book was initially published, and then across the Muslim world. Photocopies of the book's offensive passages describing Muhammad, his wives, and his Companions were circulated widely in the Muslim community.

The worldwide Muslim protest against *The Satanic Verses* was followed by the notorious *fatwa* (a legal opinion by a religious scholar)—a death sentence imposed upon Rushdie by Iran's Ayatollah Khomeini. Khomeini held that Rushdie had insulted the Prophet and was therefore an apostate whose life, according to Islamic law, should be forfeited. A reward was offered to whoever carried out the execution, and Rushdie was forced into hiding. Eventually, in order to placate the Muslim community, he converted to Islam, having previously identified himself as non-Muslim. Subsequently he changed his mind and again became a non-Muslim.

Muslim reaction to Khomeini's condemnation of Rushdie was varied. Some considered Rushdie an apostate and agreed that a price should be put on his head. Others, especially Muslim intellectuals in Western countries, strongly opposed Khomeini's fatwa and signed petitions calling for freedom of expression. A third group, among them the Nobel Laureate Naguib Mahfouz, condemned the fatwa but also criticized Rushdie's book as "intellectual terrorism," declaring that *The Satanic Verses* "is not an intellectual work . . . and a person who writes a book like this does not think; he is merely seeking consciously to insult and injure."

While it is not true that most Muslims wanted to kill Salman Rushdie, it would be wrong to think that they did not agree with the outpouring of outrage against what they considered a book intentionally written to insult their sacred beliefs and sully the image of Islam. The title *Satanic Verses* implied that the Prophet was not able to recognize malevolent "revelations" and that Islam, as its enemies have maintained, teaches that evil actions are the will of God.

The Muslim community's strong defense of Islam and the Prophet in England, where the protests started, was also an expression of great frustration with what they perceived as ill treatment by a British government that would not enlarge the British law against blasphemy (which applied only to Christianity) or allow them to establish Muslim schools in the same way that British Christian and Jewish schools had been allowed and supported by public funds.

Worldwide, what is still remembered internationally as the Rushdie affair was fueled by the gulf of misunderstanding and differences between a liberal, secular culture, which was horrified by what was seen as a medieval threat to freedom of expression, and a more conservative Muslim community, feeling disrespected, offended, and misunderstood.

# SOCIETY, POLITICS, AND ECONOMY

## *What is Islamic law?*

*Islam* means submission to the will of God. Therefore Muslims put primary emphasis on obeying God as prescribed in Islamic law. Islam's worldview is a vision of individual and communal moral responsibility; Muslims must strive or struggle (*jihad*) in the path (shariah) of God in order to implement God's will on earth, expand and defend the Muslim community, and establish a just society. The purpose of Islamic law is to provide the guidelines and requirements for two types of interactions: those between human beings and God, or worship, and those between human beings, or social transactions. Both have private and public dimensions, and both give Islam a prominent public role in Muslim community life.

Throughout history Islamic law has remained central to Muslim identity and practice, for it constitutes the ideal social blueprint for the believer who asks, "What should I do?" It is important to note that elaborating the law was the work of religious scholars (*ulama*), rather than judges, courts, or governments. The law's comprehensive coverage, including regulations ranging from religious rituals to marriage, divorce, and inheritance to setting standards for penal and international law, provided a common code of behavior and connection for all Muslim societies.

While in Christianity theology is the queen of sciences, in Islam, as in Judaism, law is the primary religious science. There is a strong distinction between Christianity's emphasis on orthodoxy (or correct doctrine or belief) and Islam's emphasis on orthopraxy (or correct action).

Sunni Muslims recognize four official sources to guide the development of Islamic law: the Quran, the Sunnah (example) of Muhammad, analogical reasoning (*qiyas*), and consensus (*ijma*). Shii accept the Quran and Sunnah as well as their own collections of traditions of Ali and other Imams whom they regard as supreme authorities and legal interpreters.

The Quranic texts provide moral directives, setting out what Muslims should aspire to as individuals and achieve as a community. The Sunnah of Muhammad (recorded in hundreds of traditions describing the Prophet's private and public life and his individual and communal activities) illustrates Islamic faith in practice and supplements and explains Quranic principles. Qiyas is used to provide parallels between similar situations or principles when no clear text is found in the Quran or Sunnah. For example, a broad prohibition of alcohol is deduced from a specific prohibition of wine, based on the altered mental state that both substances cause. The fourth source of law, ijma, originated from Muhammad's reported saying, "My community will never agree on an error." This came to mean that a consensus among religious scholars could determine permissibility of an action. Concern for justice led to the development of other legal principles that guide decision making where there are several potential outcomes. Among them were equity (*istihsan*), which permits exceptions to strict or literal legal reasoning in favor of the public interest (*maslaha*) or human welfare to assure a flexibility enabling judges to arrive at just and equitable decisions. These mechanisms allowed for multiple interpretations of texts based on context, necessity, and consensus.

Differences exist between the major Islamic law schools that reflect the diverse geographic, social, historical, and cultural contexts in which the jurists were writing. In the modern world, Islamic law faces the challenge of distinguishing the divine prescriptions and eternal principles of the Quran from regulations arising from human interpretations in response to specific historical situations. Many ulama, representing the traditional and conservative strains in Islam, continue to equate God's divinely revealed law with the laws in the legal manuals developed by the early law schools. Reformers, however, call for change in laws that are the products of social custom and human reasoning. Reformers say that what is unchanging relates to the Muslim's duties and obligations to God (worship). Laws that relate to relations with one's fellow man (social obligations), which are contingent on social and historical circumstances, are subject to change. Consequently, leaders of Islamic activist movements have reclaimed the right to *ijtihad* (independent reasoning) to reinterpret Islam to address contemporary issues and meet needs in modern societies.

Legal reforms remain a contested issue in many contemporary Muslim countries. Most Muslim states have Western-inspired legal codes addressing all areas, including the regulation of Islamic banking, which prohibits the use of interest. However, family law, which is viewed as the "heart of the Shariah" and the basis for a strong, Islamically oriented family structure and society, has remained intact in most Muslim countries. Nevertheless, significant reforms have occurred beginning in the twentieth century, most notably to protect and expand women's rights, although some scholars argue that these modern gains have not gone far enough in securing women's Quranically ordained rights.

## *What does Islamic law say about marriage, divorce, and inheritance?*

Because of the centrality of the community in Islam, the Muslim family as the basic unit of society enjoyed pride of place in the development and implementation of Islamic law. While rulers in early Islam and today might limit, circumvent, or replace penal and commercial laws, Muslim family law (the law governing marriage, divorce, and inheritance) has generally remained in force. The formulation of Muslim family law has endured for centuries but has been subject to reform and widespread debate and revision since the twentieth century.

The place of women in family law reform remains an important, extremely sensitive, and hotly contested issue in Islam. The special status of family law reflects Quranic concerns for the status and rights of women as well as the patriarchal structure of the societies in which Islamic law was developed and elaborated. The status of women and the family in Islamic law was the product of Arab culture, Quranic reforms, and foreign ideas and values assimilated from conquered peoples. The Quran introduced substantial reforms, providing new regulations and modifying local custom and practice. At the same time, much of the traditional pre-Islamic social structure with its extended family, the paramount position of males, the roles and responsibilities of its members, and family values was incorporated.

The three major areas of Muslim family law deal with marriage, divorce, and inheritance. Marriage and family life are the expected norm in Islam. In contrast to Christianity, in Islam marriage is not a sacrament but a contract between a man and a woman, or perhaps more accurately between their families. In the traditional practice of arranged marriages, the families or guardians, not the bride and groom, are the two primary actors. The preferred marriage is between two Muslims and within the extended family. In Islam, as in Judaism, marriage between first cousins has been quite common.

The Quran introduced a number of reforms that enhanced the status of women. It recognized a woman's right to contract her own marriage and receive the dower from her husband (4:4); thus she became a party to the contract, not just an object for sale. In a society where no limitations on polygamy existed, the Quran sought to control and regulate its practice, stipulating that a man could marry up to four wives provided he could support and treat them equally. It is important to note here that the Quran did not require that a man marry four wives but limited him to that number.

The relationship between a husband and wife in Islamic law is viewed as complementary, reflecting their differing characteristics, capacities, and dispositions as well as the traditional roles of men and women in the patriarchal family. The primary arena for the man is the public sphere; he is to support and protect the family. Woman's primary role is that of wife and mother, managing the household and supervising the upbringing and religious training of their children. While both are equal before God and equally required to lead virtuous lives, in family matters and society, women are subordinate because of their more sheltered and protected lives and a man's greater economic responsibilities in the extended family.

While divorce is permissible, both the Quran and Prophetic traditions underscore its seriousness. The Prophet Muhammad is reported to have said, "Of all the permitted things, divorce is the most abominable with God," and an authoritative legal manual describes divorce as "a dangerous and disapproved procedure as it dissolves marriage, . . . admitted, but on the ground of urgency of relief from an unsuitable wife."

In Arab society, men could divorce at will and on whim, and women had no grounds for divorce. The Quran and Islamic law introduced guidelines, based on greater equity and responsibility, to constrain a man's unbridled right to divorce and to establish a woman's right to a judicial (court) divorce. However, these laws were often compromised by social realities and circumvented. Thus, for example, a husband was required by law to pronounce the formula for divorce, "I divorce you," three times, once each successive month for a period of three months, during which time reconciliation was to be pursued. In fact, some men bypassed the Quranically mandated three-month waiting period (65:1) by saying, "I divorce you, I divorce you, I divorce you," three times all at one time. While Islamic law considered such an act unapproved or deviant, it was nevertheless legally valid. The force of patriarchy was especially evident in the requirement that women, in contrast to men, go before a court and present grounds to obtain a divorce.

Patriarchy also governed the rules of inheritance in pre-Islamic Arabia, according to which all property passed to the nearest male relative of the deceased. The Quran gave rights to wives, daughters, sisters, and grandmothers of the deceased, guaranteeing them a "fixed share" before the inheritance passed to the senior male. Men still inherited more than women, a fact that reflected gender relations in a male-dominated society as well as a male's greater economic responsibilities. In practice, however, Quranic and legal reforms were often circumvented by families whose women were either ignorant of their rights or intimidated into not pursuing them.

With the creation of modern nation-states in the twentieth century, many Muslim governments implemented Western-inspired legal codes. However, except in Turkey, because of religious and cultural sensitivities, family law was subject to reform rather than replacement. Islamic reformers from the late nineteenth century had called for a reinterpretation (*ijtihad*) or reformation of Islam, including modern interpretation of the Quran, to respond to the new demands of modernity and change. Among the key areas of concern were women's status and thus educational and legal reforms regarding marriage (polygamy and child marriages), divorce, and inheritance. Many governments introduced selective changes to traditional Muslim family law that ultimately entrenched state interests and power rather than protecting those whom the law targeted. The process of reform often set in motion a struggle between governments and their Western-oriented elite, who legislated or imposed change from above, and the *ulama* (scholars), who saw themselves as the defenders of Islam and its only qualified interpreters.

Reforms raised the minimum age for marriage, required that men obtain permission from a court to take a second wife or to divorce, and expanded the grounds for women to obtain a divorce. Faced with resistance to legal reforms, governments did not pursue systematic reform, and compromises were made. Often the penalties (fines or imprisonment) for failure to comply with the law were minimal. The force of religious tradition could be seen in the fact that failure to comply with reform laws rendered an act illegal but not invalid, since few governments were willing to replace Islamic law and be accused of abrogating the Shariah, or "God's law." Thus, if a man took another wife, his second marriage would be illegal and his progeny illegitimate in the eyes of the law but not invalid in the eyes of God, according to Islamic jurists.

The tenuousness of family law reforms became evident in Muslim countries such as Iran and Pakistan in recent decades as conservative ulama and Islamic movements pressed for their repeal. However, the momentum today for greater gender equality and the growing empowerment of women have increased pressure for substantive reform in many Muslim societies.

## What does Islam say about homosexuality?

Like Christians and Jews, Muslims consider sexual fulfillment within marriage for husband and wife to be the ideal state of affairs. Sex in marriage is considered a means of communication and pleasure and is not restricted to procreation. Homosexuality is considered abnormal. In some areas it is treated as a crime punishable under Islamic law, while in others homosexuality is tolerated but homosexuals are still set apart socially. Today a small minority of gay Muslims in some countries have pressed for recognition of their rights within the community.

## What does Islam say about abortion?

Muslims and Catholics find that their views regarding abortion have a lot in common. In Islam, procreation is considered to be one of the most important aspects of marriage. The Quran places a high value on life and its preservation. The Quran (17:31) says that neither poverty nor hunger should cause one to kill one's offspring. Punishment for the unlawful killing of a human being is imposed both in this life and in the next (4:93).

Muslim scholars agree that after the "ensoulment" (infusion of the soul) of the fetus (thought by some to occur at fertilization and by others after 120 days), abortion constitutes homicide and should be punished. In the case of thera-

peutic abortions for severe medical problems, a general principle of Islamic law, choosing the lesser of the two evils, has
often been applied. Rather than losing two lives, preference
is given to the life of the mother, who is the pillar of the
family with important duties and responsibilities.

## *What does Islam say about birth control?*

Islam has traditionally encouraged large families to ensure a
strong and vibrant Muslim community. The Quran does not
address family planning measures but a few *hadith* (traditions)
mention coitus interruptus. Some *ulama* (religious scholars)
oppose birth control because they believe that it opposes the
supremacy of the will of God, or that by limiting the size of
the Muslim community Islam will be weakened, or that birth
control will contribute to premarital sex and adultery.

However, the majority of ulama in the twenty-first century hold that contraception is permissible as long as both
husband and wife agree. If both agree, then the rights of both
are guaranteed. Most Muslim religious leaders oppose steril-
ization on religious grounds because it permanently alters
what God has created.

## *What does Islam say about slavery?*

Slavery, common in pre-Islamic Arabia, the Mediterranean, and
African and Asian societies, was an accepted institution in Islam
as in Judaism and Christianity. Islam did not abolish slavery
but, like Judaism and Christianity before it, set about defining it
legally and morally and moderating and mitigating the condi-
tion of slaves. Islamic law prohibited the enslavement of Muslims, non-Muslims (*dhimmi*), and orphans and foundlings who

lived within the realm of Islam (*dar al-Islam*). Only those bought or captured outside Islamic territory or the children of slaves already in captivity were recognized as legal slaves.

Slaves were recognized as persons as well as property. The emancipation of one's slaves was regarded as a meritorious act to be encouraged. Although slaves as property could be bought and sold, Islamic law prescribed that they were to be treated fairly, justly, and with kindness. They could not be killed; male slaves could not be made eunuchs, and female slaves could not be used as prostitutes. A concubine who had a child by her master would become free upon his death. Children born of a free man and a slave woman were regarded as free, not slaves. A slave mother could not be separated from her child. Slaves could marry, own property, and lead prayers.

The Abbasid Empire introduced the institution of slave soldiers (*mamluks*), which became a staple of many Muslim regimes; slave soldiers came to hold important positions in the military, becoming powerful generals and governors of provinces. In a number of important medieval Islamic states like the Mamluk sultanate in Egypt, the Delhi sultanate in India, and the Ghaznavid state in Central Asia, slave commanders became sultans or rulers. However, while some slaves became part of the social and political elite, others continued to live and labor under harsh conditions.

By the late nineteenth century, in part due to British efforts, the slave trade, especially of African slaves, declined. The Ottoman Empire officially ended slavery in 1887, although it continued to exist there and elsewhere. By the latter half of the twentieth century, slavery was abolished in Arabia and much of the Islamic world. Though slavery has been officially abolished in Islam, it can be found in Saudi Arabia, the Gulf and in the Sudan and Mauratania.

## *Why are Islamic punishments for crimes so harsh?*

Much has been written in recent years about the *hudud* punishments. Media reports from Afghanistan under the Taliban, Saudi Arabia, Iran, Sudan, and Nigeria have covered sensational stories of stonings of adulteresses and amputations of the hands and feet of thieves. Human rights activists have denounced these punishments as cruel and contrary to (Western) standards of human rights and international law. Hudud punishments had not been implemented in most modern Muslim states. However, with the rise of political Islam in the late twentieth century they were reintroduced in Pakistan, Iran, Sudan, Afghanistan, and Nigeria.

There are two broad types of punishments for crimes in Islam: *hudud* and *tazir*. Hudud refers to the "limits" or "prohibitions" of God that are explicitly defined in the Quran as punishments for specific crimes. Tazir are punishments that are at the discretion of a judge (*qadi*). These cover a wide range of penalties like fines or imprisonment.

The hudud punishments are limited to specific acts: sexual activity outside of marriage, whether fornication or adultery; false accusations of unchastity; theft; and the consumption of alcohol. The Quran indicates the crime as well as the punishment.

Crimes punishable by hudud are considered attacks against the established social order, threatening the cohesion and morality of the Muslim community. Adultery and fornication violate the order of marriage and the legal means for the procreation of children; theft violates the protection of property that is the right of every member of the community; the consumption of alcohol can lead to acts of aggression or immorality; and false accusations of unchastity—a crime already shown to carry a harsh penalty—are acts of dishonesty that damage the reputations of innocent people. It is because these acts constitute crimes against God and a threat to the moral fabric of the Muslim community that harsh punishments like flogging, stoning, and amputation have been prescribed. Strict regulations regarding evidence in cases involving hudud crimes have been established under Islamic law, and in such cases false accusations are seriously punished.

In some of the countries in which the hudud have been implemented, the excuse given is that the country had fallen into such a state of disorder and unlawfulness that very stern measures were needed to restore some semblance of social order and security. This was the case in Afghanistan under the Taliban, where after twenty years of civil war the social order had fallen into complete disarray. Other countries have used arguments similar to those used by supporters of capital punishment in the West, claiming that knowledge of harsh punishments for certain types of crimes will serve as a deterrent to the committing of those crimes. In the contemporary era, one of the most controversial aspects of stoning adulterers is that women tend to be singled out for punishment, while men are rarely punished, despite the Quranic injunction that both parties are to be punished. In countries such as Pakistan and Nigeria, a woman's pregnancy can be used as evidence against her. In cases where women report having been raped, their testimony can be, and in some cases has been, used to convict them of fornication or adultery.

Muslim reformers and critics have argued that implementation of the hudud can occur only in a society that enjoys a high degree of economic and social justice and not in societies where poverty, high unemployment, and lack of education may drive people to commit crimes of theft. Others argue that hudud punishments were appropriate within the historical and social contexts in which they originated but are inappropriate today and that the underlying religious principles and values need to find new expression in modernizing societies.

## Why don't Muslims practice a separation of church and state?

The Muslim vision of religion and politics is based upon a reading or interpretation of the Quran as well as the example of Muhammad and the early Muslim community, in tandem with the Islamic tenet that spiritual belief and action are two sides of the same coin.

Christians often cite the New Testament injunction to render unto Caesar what belongs to Caesar and to God what belongs to God as prescribing a separation of church and state. In contrast, Muslims believe that their primary act of faith is to strive to implement God's will in both their private and their public life. Throughout history, being a Muslim has meant not only belonging to a religious community of fellow believers but also living in an Islamic state governed by Islamic law (in theory if not always in practice).

Many Muslims describe Islam as a "total way of life." They believe that religion cannot be separated from social and political life, since religion informs every action that a person takes. The Quran provides many passages that emphasize the relationship of religion to state and society. It teaches that God has given the earth as a trust to humankind (2:30, 6:165). Muslims see themselves as God's representatives with a divine mandate to establish God's rule on earth in order to create a just society. The Muslim community is seen as a political entity as proclaimed in Quran 49:13, which teaches that God "made you into nations and tribes." Like Jews and Christians before them, Muslims have been called into a covenant relationship with God, making them a community of believers who must serve as an example to other nations (2:143) by creating a moral social order. "You are the best community evolved for mankind, enjoining what is right and forbidding what is wrong" (3:110).

In an ideal vision of the Islamic state, the purpose of the political authority is to implement the divine message. Thus the ideal Islamic state is a community governed by God's law (nomocracy), rather than a theocracy or autocracy that gives power to the clergy or ruler. The state should provide security and order so that Muslims can carry out their religious duties, particularly doing good and preventing evil. Legal processes implement rules and judgments from the Shariah, rather than creating new legislation. A sense of balance should exist among three groups: the caliph, who serves as the guardian of both the faith and the community; the *ulama* (religious scholars), who provide religious and legal advice; and the *qadis* (judges), who resolve disputes in accordance with Islamic law. Over time, many Muslims came to believe that this ideal blueprint and perfect state had actually existed and should be returned to. Contemporary militant movements particularly look back to this utopia as an example to be emulated today.

While a minority of Muslims today believe that modernity requires the separation of religion and the state, many Muslims continue to maintain that religion should be integral to state and society. However, there is no clear agreement—indeed, there is considerable difference of opinion—on the precise nature of the relationship of Islam to the state. For some, it is enough to say that Islam is the official state religion and that the ruler (and perhaps those who fill most senior government positions) should be Muslim. Others call for the creation of an Islamic state. But even here, there is no single agreed-upon model of government, as attested to by the diverse examples of Saudi Arabia's conservative monarchy, Iran's clergy-run state, Sudan's and Pakistan's experiments with military-imposed Islamic governments, and the Taliban's Afghanistan. And still others reject all these experiments as un-Islamic authoritarian regimes and subscribe to more secular or Islamic democratic forms of governance.

## Why does religion play such a big role in Muslim politics?

*Islam* is an Arabic word meaning "submission." A Muslim is one who submits to the will of God, one who is responsible not only for obeying God's will but also for implementing it on earth in both his or her private and public world. Being a Muslim means belonging to a worldwide community of believers (*ummah*). The responsibility of the believer to Islam and to the Muslim community overrides all other social ties and responsibilities to family, tribe, ethnicity, or nation. Politics is therefore central, since it represents the means used to carry out Islamic principles in the public sphere.

Quranic verses have been used to guide Muslim political and moral activism throughout the centuries. Twenty-first-century Islamic reformers who believe that Islam, as a comprehensive way of life, should play a central role in politics support their arguments with Quranic verses as well as the example of how Muhammad and his Companions led their lives and developed the first Muslim community. They see these primary sources and examples as a blueprint for an Islamically guided and socially just state and society.

Islam's involvement with politics dates back to its beginnings with the founding of a community-state by Muhammad in the seventh century. According to Muslim tradition, Muhammad's first successor, Abu Bakr, was challenged by several Arab tribes, who argued that the death of Muhammad represented the end of their political allegiance to the broader Muslim community. However, Abu Bakr reminded the Arab tribes of the overarching message of Islam—that membership in and loyalty to the Muslim community transcended all tribal bonds, customs, and traditions. Abu Bakr did not accept the argument of the Arab tribes that religion and politics were two separate and unrelated entities. Rather, he said, religion was intended to guide political decisions and to provide legitimacy to a political system. All Muslims belong to a single community whose unity is based upon the interconnection of religion and the state, where faith and politics are inseparable.

Under the political leadership of Muhammad and his successors, Islam expanded from what is now Saudi Arabia into Islamic empires and cultures that stretch across North Africa, through the Middle East and into Asia and Europe. Historically Islam has served as the religious ideology for the foundation of a variety of Muslim states, including the great Islamic empires: Umayyad (661–750), Abbasid (750–1258), Ottoman (1281–1924), Safavid (1501–1722), and Mughal (1526–1857). In each of these empires and other sultanate states, Islam informed the state's legal, political, educational, and social institutions.

Today, Islam's connection with politics varies by country and region, but there are several common reasons why religion is intimately connected to the state. First of all, by the nineteenth century most Muslim countries were in a state of internal decline, and they were vulnerable to European imperialism. Muslims experienced the defeats of their societies at the hands of Christian Europe as a religious as well as political and cultural crisis. This crisis was deepened by Christian missionaries who attributed their conquests not only to superior military technology and economic power but also to the superiority of Western Christian civilization and religion. Because religion took on these political overtones on the part of Western colonialists, it is not surprising that some Muslims looked to the combination of religion and politics for a solution. Muslim responses to European colonialism ranged from resistance or struggle, justified as jihad in the defense of Islam in the face of the Christian onslaught, to accommodation and/or assimilation with the West.

Second, in the twentieth century many Muslim societies experienced a widespread feeling of failure and loss of self-esteem. The achievement of independence from colonial rulers in the mid-twentieth century created high expectations that have not been realized. Muslims have suffered from failed political systems and economies and the negative effects of modernization: overcrowded cities lacking social support systems, high unemployment, government corruption, and a growing gap between rich and poor. Rather than leading to a better quality of life, modernization has been associated with a breakdown of traditional family, religious, and social values. Many Muslims blame Western models of political and economic development as sources of moral decline and spiritual malaise.

Third, when Muslims ask themselves what went wrong, for many the inevitable answer is that their societies have strayed from the straight path of Islam that had led them to great development and success historically. Therefore future success depends upon returning to a society whose politics are governed by Islam.

## *Why do Muslims reject secularism?*

Muslim reactions to the term *secularism* have been influenced by Western history, politics, and religion, as well as by fear that secularism leads to the marginalization of religion. The term *secularism* has often been misunderstood and seen as diametrically opposed to *religion*. European colonialism and attempts to introduce modernity were interpreted by Muslims as an attempt to impose Western secularism, separating religion from state and society and thus weakening the moral fabric of Muslim society. While some Muslims, especially among the Western-oriented elites, believed that secularism was necessary to build strong modern societies, many others saw it as a direct challenge to Islam and its heritage, in which religion had for centuries been closely associated with successful and powerful empires. Secularism was equated with unbelief and thus seen as a direct threat to the religious identity and values of Muslim societies.

The problem was compounded by the fact that Muslim languages lacked a precise equivalent word for modern secularism. Few have understood that American secularism separated religion and the state to avoid privileging any one religion and to guarantee freedom of belief or unbelief to all. Little notice was taken of the diverse forms that secularism has taken in modern Western secular countries like Britain, Germany, and Canada that have a state religion and provide state support for recognized religions.

The examples of France and Turkey, which have been anticlerical and have banned the wearing of Muslim headscarves in their schools, reinforce the belief that secularism means a state that is antireligious rather than simply religiously neutral. On the other hand, in recent years many Muslims in

Turkey and India have called for a "true" secular state, one that does not privilege any religion but ensures freedom of religious belief and practice.

## Why is Jerusalem so important to Muslims?

Jerusalem is revered as a holy city by all three of the great monotheistic faiths. The importance of Jerusalem to the early Islamic community is seen in the fact that Jerusalem was the original *qibla* (location that all Muslims face when they pray). In addition, according to tradition, Jerusalem was the Prophet's destination in his Night Journey from Mecca, when he traveled with Gabriel to see everything in heaven and earth and to the Temple in Jerusalem, where he met with Abraham, Moses, Jesus, and other prophets. The Night Journey made Jerusalem the third holiest city in Islam and affirmed the continuity of Islam with Judaism and Christianity.

Today Muslims view the creation of the state of Israel and the declaration of Jerusalem as its capital as reminders of the injustices of Western imperialism and powerful symbols of the continuing weakness of contemporary Muslim societies. The history of Jerusalem helps us to see the role the city has played in all three monotheistic faiths.

Jerusalem was originally a Canaanite settlement where, according to the Hebrew scripture, David, King of Israel, built his capital and his son Solomon built the Temple. Muslim armies took Jerusalem without resistance in 635 and immediately began to refurbish its chief holy place, the neglected Temple Mount of the "noble sanctuary." First the congregational mosque al-Aqsa was built, and then the magnificent shrine the "Dome of the Rock" was completed by 692. The Dome is thought to be the destination of Muhammad's Night

Journey as well as the biblical site of Abraham's sacrifice and Solomon's Temple.

During this period, Jerusalem was home to many Christians and to Jews who had been permitted by the Muslims to return to the city for the first time since their ban by the Romans in 135. Both Jews and Christians may have outnumbered the Muslims in Jerusalem at this time. The city's history was generally uneventful until the Crusades.

One event that provoked the Crusaders' invasion of Palestine in 1099 and the occupation of Jerusalem was the burning of the Christians' Holy Sepulchre Church by the Egyptian ruler al-Hakim bi-amr Alah. During the eighty-eight-year Latin Christian occupation of Jerusalem, the Crusaders converted the Dome of the Rock into a church and al-Aqsa into the headquarters of the Knights Templar. When Salah al-Din (Saladin) drove them out in 1187, he restored the Muslim holy places to their original use and, aided by popular preachers, raised Muslim appreciation of this third holiest city in Islam, after Mecca and Medina.

Salah al-Din's successors, the Mamluks and then the Ottomans, generously supported the city, which thrived until the disintegration of the Ottoman empire in the nineteenth century. In the First World War Turkey joined Germany against the Allies, and Jerusalem fell to the British in 1917. When the British withdrew in 1948, the Jordanians occupied the Old City, and it remained a part of Jordan until the 1967 war, when Israel took it over.

What is called the Arab world's "Six Day War" with Israel (it was actually more like a six-hour war) and the devastating failure of the combined forces of Egypt, Syria, and Jordan against tiny Israel came to be remembered in Arab literature as "the disaster." It transformed the Arab and Palestinian problem into an Islamic issue. The loss of Jerusalem and its sacred shrines was a major blow to Muslim pride, faith, and identity. The "liberation of Jerusalem" became a worldwide Islamic slogan and Muslim cause.

## Is Islam compatible with democracy?

All the world's religions in premodern times supported monarchies and feudal societies, then moved to accommodate modern forms of democracy. Similarly, Muslims today are debating the relationship of Islam to democracy. While most Muslims wish for greater political participation, the rule of law, government accountability, freedoms, and human rights, there are many different ways to achieve these goals.

There are many reactions to democratization in the Muslim world. Some, from the late King Fahd of Saudi Arabia to ultra-conservatives and extremists, argue that Islam has its own mechanisms and institutions, which do not include democracy. Others believe that democracy can fully be realized only if Muslim societies restrict religion to private life. Still others contend that Islam is fully capable of accommodating and supporting democracy. Engaging in a process of reform, they argue the compatibility between Islam and democracy by using traditional Islamic concepts like consultation (*shura*) between ruler and ruled, community consensus (*ijma*), public interest (*maslaha*), and *ijtihad* (the use of human reason to reinterpret Islamic principles and values and to meet the new needs of society). These mechanisms can be used to support parliamentary forms of government with systems of checks and balances among the executive, legislative, and judiciary branches.

Many believe that just as the modern democracies of America and Europe accommodate diverse relationships with religion, so too Muslims can develop their own forms of democratic states that are responsive to indigenous values. However, rulers of authoritarian states tend to ignore, discourage, or suppress movements for democratization.

## Why aren't Muslim countries more democratic?

Unelected governments whose leaders are kings, military, and ex-military rule the majority of countries in the Muslim world. However, in recent years competitive elections have occurred in countries like Indonesia, Bangladesh, Turkey, and Senegal. The absence of democracy in the Muslim world today has led many to ask whether there is something about Arab or Muslim culture that is antithetical to democracy. The answer to this question lies more in history and politics than in religion.

While the West has had centuries to make its transformation from monarchies and principalities to modern democratic states, a process that was marked by revolutionary and civil wars, the Muslim world has struggled with several centuries of colonial rule followed by authoritarian regimes installed by European powers. If we ask why much of the Muslim world today is underdeveloped or unstable, we must remember that most modern Muslim states are only several decades old and that they were carved out by European powers.

In South Asia, the British divided the Indian subcontinent into India and Pakistan, giving portions of the Muslim-majority state of Kashmir to each of them. The conflicts that resulted from these actions have led to the deaths of millions in communal warfare between Hindus and Muslims, the civil war between East and West Pakistan that led to the creation of Bangladesh, and conflicts in Kashmir over Indian rule that persist to the present day. In the Middle East, the French created modern Lebanon from portions of Syria, and the British set the borders for Iraq and Kuwait and created the totally new country of Jordan. Such arbitrary borders fed ethnic, regional, and religious conflicts including the Lebanese Civil War between Christians and Muslims, the occupation of Lebanon by Syria, and the Gulf War, which resulted from Saddam Hussein's claim to Kuwaiti territory.

In addition to influencing who came to power in emerging modern Muslim nation-states, Europe and later America forged close alliances with authoritarian regimes, tolerating or supporting their nondemocratic ways in exchange for their allegiance during the Cold War or to ensure our access to oil.

Not surprisingly, Muslim rulers have been plagued with issues of identity and legitimacy. The artificial nature of many modern states and the weak legitimacy of rulers have resulted in nondemocratic governments, societies in which state power is heavily reliant on security forces, police, and military, and where freedoms of assembly, speech, and press are severely limited. Many Muslim states operate within a culture of authoritarianism that is opposed to democratization, civil society, independent political parties, trade unions, and a free press. When useful, some rulers use religion to legitimate themselves and their policies. At other times, as during the aftermath of crises like the Gulf War of 1991 and the World Trade Center and Pentagon attacks of September 11, 2001, they also use the threat of "Islamic extremism" to justify increased suppression or repression of any and all opposition to their undemocratic rule.

## *Why does Islam reject capitalism?*

Islam has no problem with many of the essentials of capitalism. It is important to remember that Muhammad, the preeminent model for all Muslims, was a prosperous businessman who engaged in financial and commercial transactions to make a living and that his earliest followers included successful merchants. The Quran as well as Muslim historical experience confirms the right to private property, trade, and commerce.

Mosques throughout the world, like the Umayyad mosque in Damascus and the grand mosques in old Cairo and Tehran, are often adjoined by magnificent bazaars. Traders and businessmen constituted one of the most successful sectors in Muslim society and were often responsible for the spread of their faith.

Capitalism exists both in its homegrown forms in the Muslim world and in Western-inspired versions. However, many in the Muslim world, like many in other parts of the world, are concerned about the dark side of capitalism, the possible abuses of a free market economy including the seeming lack of concern for the poor and weaker sectors of society. More specifically, they fear forces of a globalization will lead to greater Western economic penetration in Muslim countries. The result, they fear, will be continued Muslim dependence on the West and a free market economy that is geared only toward maximizing profits, which may increase the growing gap between rich and poor. Finally, they fear a contagious Western culture whose retail stores, advertising, music, media, and dress can erode traditional Muslim religious ideals and threaten the identity and values of Muslim youth.

However, given an even playing field, perhaps the best response to those who ask whether Islam and capitalism are compatible is to look at the lives of the millions of Muslims who live and work in our midst in America and Europe. Many have come here to enjoy our freedoms and the opportunities offered by our economic as well as our political systems. Like other religious and ethnic minorities before them, they too struggle with issues of identity and assimilation but not with their desire to enjoy the best that we represent.

## *What does Islam have to say about poverty and social justice?*

One of the most striking and controversial elements of the Quran at the time when it was revealed was its firm commitment to social justice, a significant threat to the tribal power structures in place. Rather than accepting the principle that the strongest are the most powerful, the Quran emphasized the responsibility of Muslims to care for and protect one another, regardless of socioeconomic status. In fact, the Quran repeatedly emphasizes the need to care especially for those who were outcasts under the tribal system—widows, orphans, and the poor. One way of doing this was through *zakat* (almsgiving), which is one of the Five Pillars of Islam. Zakat consists of giving 2.5 percent of one's total wealth annually to support the less fortunate. In addition, usury, or the collection of interest, was forbidden because it served as a means of exploiting the poor. False contracts were also denounced. The Quran and Sunnah (example of the Prophet) further give Muslims permission to engage in armed defense of downtrodden men, women, and children (Quran 4:74–76) and those who have been wronged, particularly those who have been driven out of their homes unjustly (22:39–40).

Through all of these declarations, the Quran emphasized the responsibility of the rich toward the poor and dispossessed. The new social order called for by the Quran reflected the fact that the purpose of all actions was the fulfillment of God's will, not following the desires of tribes or of self. By asserting that all believers belong to a single universal community (*ummah*),

Muhammad sought to break the bonds of tribalism and place Muslims under a single prophetic leader and authority.

Issues of social justice came to the forefront of Muslim societies in the early twentieth century with the rise of industrialism. The influx of large numbers of peasants from the countryside into urban areas created social and demographic tensions that led to a crisis, particularly in Egypt. The Egyptian Muslim Brotherhood, founded in 1928, proposed Islam as the organizational and religious solution to poverty and assistance to the dispossessed and downtrodden. Its founder, Hasan al-Banna, taught a message of social and economic justice, preaching particularly to the poor and uneducated. In al-Banna's vision, Islam was not just a philosophy, religion, or cultural trend but a social movement seeking to improve all areas of life, not only those that were inherently religious. That is, rather than being simply a belief system, Islam was a call to social action.

Another major ideologue of social justice was the Egyptian Muslim Brother Sayyid Qutb, who later became the ideologue of radical Islam. According to Qutb, Islam's understanding of social justice takes account of both the material and spiritual well-being of a person. It promotes the absolute equality of all people in the eyes of God. It calls for freedom of conscience and emphasizes the permanent responsibilities of all Muslims toward society. This combination of material and spiritual welfare recognizes that those who are hungry or who have no shelter cannot attend to spiritual matters because they are necessarily preoccupied by the struggle for daily survival. In order for a person to be capable of attention to more spiritual concerns, the absolute necessities of daily life must be provided. Therefore, one of the major responsibilities of the Muslim community must be the eradication of poverty. By caring for their poor, Muslims as individuals and the Muslim community collectively demonstrate their concern and care for their own. It is in this spirit that zakat should be understood. It is a required social responsibility intended to combat poverty and to prevent the wealthy from accumulating and holding onto all of their wealth while the poor remain poor. The redistribution of wealth is intended to break the cycle of poverty and to verify that the daily necessities of all Muslims are cared for. This redistribution of wealth also underscores the Muslim belief that everything ultimately belongs to God. Human beings are simply caretakers, or vicegerents, for God's property. The redistribution of wealth, therefore, is really about a fairer allocation of God's resources within the broader community.

In the contemporary era, the Islamist emphasis on Islam's message of social justice has been particularly powerful in gaining adherents from poorer and less advantaged groups, particularly in Israel-Palestine and Lebanon. Groups like Hamas and Hizbollah devote most of their budgets to social welfare activities and call for the empowerment of the poor and weak. Like Christian liberation theologians, they teach that social justice can only be achieved if the poor rise up against their oppressive conditions.

## *Why does Islam prohibit the charging of interest?*

Opposition to the use of interest originates in Quranic verses that prohibit usury or *riba*, an ancient Arabian practice that doubles the debt of borrowers who default on their loans and doubles it again if they default a second time. Those opposed to interest cite the Quranic prohibition against riba and argue that interest gives an unfair gain to the lender, who receives money without working for it, and imposes an unfair burden on the borrower, who must repay the loan and a finance charge regardless of whether his money grows or he suffers a monetary loss. They also believe that interest transfers wealth from poor to rich, promotes selfishness, and weakens community bonds.

In the twenty-first century, controversy about the use of interest continues. Some believe that interest paid by government bonds and regular savings accounts does not violate the spirit of Islam, while others see all interest as socially unjust. A number of Islamic banks (see next question) have been created in recent years based upon mechanisms that employ borrowing and lending on a profit- and loss-sharing basis, paying no interest on deposits and charging no interest on loans. It is too early to predict the long-term success of these experiments, but these alternatives to conventional lending have been welcomed enthusiastically by many who are motivated by moral rather than strictly financial concerns.

## *What is Islamic banking?*

Modern banking was established in the Muslim world in the mid-nineteenth century. Early commercial banks were influenced and owned by Europeans. By the end of the twentieth century, Muslim-owned banks emerged throughout the Muslim world. However, modern Western-inspired interest-based banking remained controversial for many religious leaders.

Because Muslim tradition maintains that the Quran forbids the taking or charging of interest (*riba*), many Muslims are uncomfortable with conventional banks which both charge interest on loans and pay interest on savings accounts. Although some reformers today insist that *riba* in the Quran refers to usury, not modern banking interest, the traditional historical equation of riba with interest prevails.

The Quranic prohibition of interest is based upon the assertion that the charging of interest on loans is a means of exploiting the poor. In other words, the charging of interest on money loaned increases the financial hardship of the person borrowing the money. Furthermore, the practice of conventional savings is equated with the hoarding of wealth in the expectation of a predetermined return with no risk to the investor.

The concept of commercial Islamic banking, that is, banking in which interest is neither charged nor paid, dates to the 1920s when a group of Muslim businessmen realized that traditional means of conducting financial transactions were no longer sufficient for doing business in modern economies. In particular, Islamic banks were founded to fund trading activity. The first modern Islamic banking institutions were farmer credit unions founded in Pakistan in the 1950s and a small rural institution founded in Egypt in 1963. Islamic banking expanded in the 1970s with the founding of the Dubai Islamic Bank (1975), the Faysal Islamic Banks in Egypt and Sudan and the Kuwait Finance House (1977), the Jordan Islamic Bank (1978), and the Bahrain Islamic Bank (1978). Islamic banking then spread to Malaysia and Indonesia. Since the 1970s, some commercial banks in both Muslim countries and Europe have begun offering Islamic banking services. Islamic financial instruments are increasingly accepted internationally, even in non-Muslim countries.

Islamic banks charge fees for services for their accounts rather than interest. Savings accounts do not earn interest. However, it is possible for bank patrons to participate in bank investments and either earn a share of the profit on the return or suffer a portion of the losses sustained by the bank. These transactions are permissible under Islamic law because they involve a degree of risk on the part of the investor.

The principle of profit-sharing (*mudarabah*) is well established in Islam. Under a profit-sharing agreement, the depositor has the option of earning a share either in the bank's general profits or in the profits from a specified investment or series of investments. The depositor generally places money in an "investment account" (as opposed to a "savings account"). The rate of profit is declared by the bank at the end of the fiscal year. In cases where the bank suffers a loss, no profit shares are paid out. However, the value of the deposits is usually guaranteed, although equity is not, since the value of the equity is determined by the stock market.

Like conventional banks, Islamic banks offer current account facilities, such as checking accounts and demand deposit accounts, which can be accessed either by writing checks or by ATMs. International charge cards, such as Visa, may be offered but are strictly debit cards rather than credit cards. Consequently, only current account holders are eligible for charge cards. Long-term credit is available through leasing and installment sales in which the customer pays a certain amount monthly and ultimately takes ownership of the item. Longer-term financing through an Islamic bank is also possible in an arrangement in which the bank serves as a partner in the business. In such a case, the bank may either provide funding only or a combination of funding and management and entrepreneurial skills. An Islamic bank can further enter into an equity-sharing arrangement (*musharakah*) with a company.

In addition to satisfying the ethical concerns of many Muslims seeking to do business and to save money, Islamic banking has also provided an alternative model for financing for developing countries. The use of equity-sharing, rather than debt financing, is considered to be a more positive means of helping developing countries carry out their long-term planning and encourages greater foreign investment.

# MUSLIMS IN THE WEST

## *Who are the Muslims of America?*

Although estimates of the number of American Muslims vary considerably from four to twelve million, it is safe to say that there are at least four to six million, making Islam the third largest religion (after Christianity and Judaism) in America. This means that there are more Muslims in America than Episcopalians. Many believe that in the first half of the twenty-first century Islam will become the second largest religion in America.

Muslims were present in America before the nineteenth century. The explorers, traders, and settlers who visited the New World from the time of Columbus included Muslims. Moriscos (Spanish Muslims who hid their Muslim faith) migrated to both Spanish and Portuguese settlements in America. In addition, between 14 percent and 20 percent of the African slaves brought to America between the sixteenth and nineteenth centuries were Muslim, although they were forced to convert to Christianity. Other Muslims, particularly Indians and Arabs, who were not slaves also immigrated during this period and were able to maintain their spiritual, cultural, and social identity.

The numbers of Muslims in America increased in the late nineteenth century with the arrival of significant numbers of immigrants from the Arab world (Syria, Lebanon, and Jordan). Many settled in the Midwest and Canada as blue-collar workers and assimilated into American society. After World War II, significant numbers of immigrants from Palestine, who had lost their homes after the creation of Israel in 1948, and elites from the Middle East and South Asia, who sought either an education or professional advancement, came to America. In recent decades, many students from the Muslim world have come to study, and many well-educated professionals and intellectuals have come from South and Southeast Asia as well as from the Middle East for political and economic reasons. Many Muslim immigrants have worked hard to sustain and pass down their Islamic identity to their children and to establish institutions and community structures—including mosques, Islamic centers, Islamic schools, Islamic publication organizations, interest-free financial institutions, and charitable organizations to support these goals.

African-American Islam originated with the Nation of Islam in 1930. Initially it differed significantly from mainstream Islam in its doctrines of black militancy and separatism and its theology. (See page 52, "Is there a difference between Muslims and Black Muslims?") The Nation did not follow the major Muslim rituals or the Five Pillars of Islam.

Since the mid-1970s, under the leadership of Warith Deen Muhammad the bulk of the Nation of Islam has been integrated into mainstream Islam. Temples were renamed *masjids* or mosques, and their leaders were called imams rather than ministers; the community observed the Five Pillars of Islam (profession of faith, prayer, fasting, *zakat*, and pilgrimage) in union with the worldwide Islamic community of which they were now members; black separatist doctrines were dropped as the community began to participate within the political process and system; the equality of men and women believers was reaffirmed, and women were given more responsible positions in the ministry of the community.

The transformation of the Nation of Islam under Warith Deen Muhammad did not occur without dissent. While the majority of the Nation's temples and ministers accepted Wallace and his reforms, a minority under the leadership of Louis Farrakhan did not. Maintaining that he and his followers had remained faithful to the message and mission of Elijah Muhammad, Farrakhan claimed the mantle of leadership of the Nation of Islam. Minister Farrakhan retained the name and organizational structure of the Nation of Islam as well as its black nationalist and separatist doctrines. However, in recent years, he has moved the Nation closer to more orthodox Islàmic practices and declared that he now sees his movement within the mainstream Islam. Time will tell whether this transformation proves genuine.

About two-thirds of the Muslims in America today are immigrants or descendants of immigrants. The other third is made up of African-American converts to Islam along with smaller numbers of white American converts and Hispanic Muslims. The largest Muslim communities in the United States are in Boston, New York City, Detroit, Dearborn, Toledo, Chicago, Houston, and Los Angeles/Orange County.

## What kinds of problems do Muslims face in America?

Only a few decades ago, Muslims were mostly invisible in the West. There was little awareness of the presence or relevance of Islam in Western societies. Greater consciousness of Islam emerged principally as a result of conflicts such as the Iranian revolution, as well as hijackings and hostage taking in Lebanon, the Gulf, and Pakistan. Some saw these events as signs of an Islamic threat or a clash of civilizations, Islam versus the West. America's relationship with Muslims was seen within a context of conflict and confrontation. Islam was viewed as a foreign religion, distinct from the Judeo-Christian tradition. This reinforced a sense of "us" and "them." Subsequent attacks against America and Americans in Somalia, Saudi Arabia, and Africa, and most recently in New York and Washington on 9/11, have led many to regard Muslims with fear and distrust. They judge Islam as inherently violent and militant, religiously and culturally.

Like many other immigrants of diverse religious and ethnic backgrounds, Muslims have been challenged to define their place in American and European society. In trying to do this, like other religious minorities before them such as Jews and Catholics, they struggle with the relationship of faith to national identity (assimilation, integration, multiculturalism), intermarriage, gender relations, worship, and education. Many struggle with the English language, as well as their desire to hold on to their native or homeland cultures, and many face religious and ethnic discrimination in the workplace and society. Ironically, many of the minorities who preceded them and "made it in America" do not identify with what Muslims are now facing. They fail to see the similarities between their own past and Muslims' current problems. There are many reasons for this. Muslims fall outside the circle of American pluralism. However different previous religious and ethnic minorities may have been, the vast majority were Judeo-Christian. Most regard Islam as a thoroughly foreign religion. Few think of it as an Abrahamic religion, part of a Judeo-Christian-Islamic tradition. In the absence of this knowledge and awareness, Islam is often seen through explosive "headline events," and thus the hatred and violence of a minority of religious extremists obscure the faith of the mainstream majority.

Like Jewish law for Jews, adherence to Islamic law is an important point of faith for Muslims. Islamic law covers many aspects of life: religious requirements, dietary regulations, and family law. Many Muslims have had to make special arrangements to attend their Friday congregational prayer at a mosque or Islamic center, a worship obligation that is comparable to the Jewish Sabbath or Christian service on Sunday, or to arrange the time and place to pray while they are at work or school. Dietary regulations, particularly the requirement to eat meat that has been slaughtered in a religiously appropriate way (*halal*) and not to eat pork products, are often difficult to follow in an American setting. A halal butcher shop may not be available, and American food manufacturers and restaurants often use pork-based products, particularly lard, to prepare food. Many Muslims who have not been able to find halal meat shops have turned instead to Jewish kosher butchers.

In recent years a major issue for Muslims has been the Americanization of the Muslim experience. Although in the past imams and other religious teachers were brought in from foreign countries, there is increasing recognition that these imams are not always aware of or sensitive to the problems of daily life that American Muslims encounter. Consequently, training of "native" imams has been seriously undertaken since the 1980s. In addition, legal councils specifically addressing life in America have been founded to respond to questions raised by communities here. Another major development since the 1980s has been the effort made by Muslims to participate in interfaith activities with Jews and Christians.

Living as a minority in a dominant culture that is often ignorant about Islam or even hostile to it, many Muslims experience a sense of marginalization, alienation, and powerlessness. Some Muslims are further marked as "different" by their manner of dress, particularly women who veil and men who wear beards and skullcaps or turbans, and they are sometimes singled out for harassment. This has increasingly been the case since September 11, 2001.

Despite problems, however, Muslims, long regarded as "other," are now part of the fabric of our society, as neighbors, co-workers, citizens, and believers. Muslims have increasingly become more integrated into the American political process both as individuals and organizationally. A host of national and international organizations have been created to monitor and promote Muslim causes and interests. Among the more prominent are the American Muslim Council (AMC), the Council for American Islamic Relations (CAIR), the Muslim Public Affairs Council (MPAC), the Islamic Circle of North America (ICNA), the Islamic Society of North America (ISNA), and the Center for the Study of Islam and Democracy (CSID).

Muslims and non-Muslims in the West face a common challenge of pluralism and tolerance. Too often in the past tolerance has meant "suffering" the existence of others while regarding them as inferior. Today, all are challenged to embrace a modern form of pluralism and tolerance based upon mutual understanding and respect. To affirm the truth of one's own religion or worldview does not exclude the ability to acknowledge principles and values shared with others. Recognition of significant religious differences can still be accompanied by respect for the rights of others to hold different religious beliefs.

## *Who and where are the Muslims of Europe?*

The presence of Muslims in European areas is not a new development. From the eighth century to the fifteenth, Muslims ruled Spain and areas of southern Italy and southern France. During the eleventh century, Muslims also existed as a minority under Christian rulers who sold them as slaves, a practice that in fact continued until the nineteenth century. While many have been taught that in 1492 Isabella sent Christopher Columbus off to the New World, few are equally aware that 1492 also marks the fall of Granada and the beginning of a campaign to drive the Muslims (Moors) out of Spain and Western Europe. By the seventeenth century, most Muslims, along with Jews, who were also persecuted as heretics, had fled to North Africa.

Estimates of the number of Muslims now residing in Western Europe range from ten to fifteen million. The ethnic diversity of Muslims in Europe is extremely broad, representing most of the major ethnic groups of the Muslim world. Most numerous are Turks, Algerians, Moroccans, and then Pakistanis. Because of this great diversity, despite a common religious bond, it is difficult to speak of a homogenous Muslim community in any individual country, let alone across Europe.

Muslims may be found in significant numbers in most Western European countries. The largest Muslim populations are to be found in France, Germany, and the United Kingdom, followed by smaller communities in such countries as Belgium, Spain, the Netherlands, Sweden, Denmark, Norway, and Austria.

Although some immigration to Britain and France began before World War II, the major waves of Muslim migration came afterward. In contrast to America, whose Muslim population is heavily indebted to family- or village-based immigration, educational migration, and the growth of Islam among the African-American community, the Muslim presence in Europe is due in large part to labor immigration and a vestigial colonial connection.

When their countries achieved independence, many of those Muslims who had cooperated with European colonizers chose to emigrate. Professionals and skilled laborers from former European colonies in Africa, South Asia, and the Arab world emigrated to Europe seeking a better life. Then, in the 1960s and 1970s, unskilled laborers flooded into a Europe whose growing economies were in need of cheap labor. More than a million Muslims, many from France's former North African and West African colonies, were admitted to France alone. Germany and Britain had similar stories. From the 1970s onward, increasing numbers of Muslim students came to Europe, as they did to America, to study. While many returned home as trained physicians, engineers, scientists, and teachers, others, for political or economic reasons, chose to stay.

France has the largest Muslim population in Europe. Its five million Muslims, including thirty-five thousand converts, account for almost 10 percent of the population. They may be found in most major cities and towns. The Muslims of France now outnumber Protestants and Jews and are second only to Roman Catholics. There are grand mosques in major cities like Paris and Lyons and more than a thousand mosques and prayer rooms throughout the country. Muslim communities have continued to grow because of their high birth rate, regulations that permit additional immigration to reunite families, and a continual flow of legal and illegal entrants from North Africa.

Britain's one to two million Muslims come primarily from the Indian subcontinent, although others are from Africa,

Malaysia, and the Arab world. They are concentrated in the northern industrial cities of Bradford, Birmingham, and Leeds and in the East End of London. More than six hundred mosques serve as prayer, education, and community centers, many of which have been built with funds from the Middle East, particularly Saudi Arabia. In contrast to France and Germany, where most Muslims do not have the right to vote, most Muslims in Britain come from British Commonwealth countries and thus have enjoyed British citizenship and full participation in political life, as voters and as candidates; indeed some have been elected to political office. There are three Muslims in the House of Lords and two in the House of Commons. Muslims are also involved in local government; it is estimated that more than two hundred serve as councillors. Even more Muslims have been elected to the Dutch parliament's equivalent of the House of Commons. By contrast, in France and Spain there are no Muslim representatives in the national legislature, and only one in Germany.

## *What are the issues that European Muslims face?*

However different their experiences may be, Muslims in Europe and in America have common concerns regarding the practice of their faith, the retention of Islamic identity (in particular for their children), and the preservation of family life and values. Specific concerns include the ability to take time out from work to pray daily, to attend mosque on Friday for the weekly congregational prayer, and to celebrate the two great feasts of Islam (Eid al-Adha and Eid al-Fitr), the availability of *halal* foods in schools and the military, and, for those women who wish, the right to wear a headscarf (*hijab*). Some request segregated athletics classes and are concerned about coeducation, sex education, especially regarding the issue of homosexuality, and secularism in the schools.

The issue of assimilation has been particularly acute in France, where after a long battle the government has taken a firm stand on full integration rather than the multicultural approaches of Britain and America. In a celebrated case, France, in contrast to Britain and most countries in the West, outlawed the wearing of a headscarf by female students. Both France's ministry of education and its teachers' unions were united in claiming that the hijab violated France's secular constitution and traditions. After several years of bitter debate, the French Constitutional Council ruled in October 1996 that despite the education ministry's ban, students could not be expelled for wearing headscarves if no proselytizing occurred.

The Muslim experience in France has been affected negatively by the rise of right-wing nationalism with its antiforeign rhetoric and agenda. A foreign labor force, welcomed during a period of economic expansion, became a convenient scapegoat, charged with stealing "French jobs." Amidst growing unemployment, Jean-Marie Le Pen's National Front advocated the forced expulsion of three million immigrants, as well as priority for native French in jobs, housing, and welfare benefits.

At the same time, many North Africans from Morocco, Tunisia, and Algeria have entered France, legally and illegally. In particular, the civil war in Algeria caused many Algerians to flee to France, swelling the ranks of its already sizeable North African population. After the Islamic Salvation Front (FIS) swept first Algerian municipal elections and the parliamentary elections in the early 1990s, the military stepped in, seized power, canceled a second round of parliamentary elections, and denied the FIS their parliamentary victory, charging that the Islamists were out to use elections to "hijack democracy." In the aftermath, the government arrested thousands of FIS members and repressed the movement. In the ensuing spiral of violence and counterviolence, which claimed more than one hundred thousand lives, moderates became radicalized, and extremist groups like the Armed Islamic Group and, within the military, the *eradicateurs* emerged.

Bombings in Paris attributed to Algeria's radical Armed Islamic Group, increased concern about al-Qaeda terrorists, and a rash of attacks against synagogues have contributed to questions about Islam's compatibility with French culture, Judeo-Christian or secular, and whether Muslims could be true and loyal citizens of France.

At the heart of the French debate has been a tendency to see Islam as a foreign religion, placing it over and against the Judeo-Christian tradition. While many have insisted upon a process of acculturation that left little room for a multicultural approach, others have argued that Muslims should be allowed to develop a distinct French Muslim identity that blends established French principles and values with Islamic faith and values.

Post 9/11, the impact of the attacks in New York and Washington and Madrid and London have increased Islamophobia, hate crimes and discrimination. New anti-terrorism legislation has raised concerns that the legislation goes beyond targeting violent extremists and eradicating or containing terrorism and threatens the civil liberties of mainstream Muslims in Europe and America. At the same time, Muslims have been challenged to more publicly and forcefully address the sources of religious extremism, to marginalize and discredit terrorists like Osama Bin Laden, to denounce acts of extremism and terrorism.

Muslims in Europe, as in America, face issues that relate to their minority status: issues of citizenship in non-Muslim territories and participation in political and public life, the status and role of women in the family and community, religious pluralism, and secularism. Some estimates indicate that Muslims will outnumber non-Muslims in part of Europe by 2050. In many of the major European cities, however, given the low birthrates of indigenous populations, Muslim schoolchildren will be in the majority within the next decade. Obviously, coexistence of Muslims and non-Muslims is here to stay. All are challenged to move beyond stereotypes and established patterns of behavior to a more inclusive and pluralistic vision informed by a multi-dimensional dialogue, to build a future based upon mutual understanding and respect.

# GLOSSARY

**adhan**  Muslim call to prayer.

**Agha Khan**  Leader of the Nizari Ismaili sect of Shii Muslims who oversees cultural and spiritual lives of followers.

**Aisha**  Muhammad's influential wife, daughter of the first Sunni caliph, acknowledged authority on history, medicine, poetry, and rhetoric, and one of the most important transmitters of *hadith*.

**Ali**  Muhammad's cousin and son-in-law (married to Muhammad's daughter Fatima). Shii Muslims believe that Ali was the first caliph to succeed Muhammad (Sunnis place him fourth). Shiis trace the ruling descendants of Muhammad (Imams) through him.

**Allah**  God.

**Allahu Akbar**  Literally, "God is most great." Phrase used for Muslim call to prayer.

**Assassins**  Eponym given to the Nizari Ismaili sect of Shii Muslims due to campaign of terror and violence, including assassinations, they carried out against the Sunni Seljuq Dynasty in the name of the Hidden Imam. Last grand master was executed in 1256 C.E.

**ayatollah**  Literally, "sign of God." Highest rank of Shii Muslim clerics. Respected for knowledge and piety.

**bayah**  Oath of allegiance.

**bida**  Innovation or unacceptable departure from the example of Muhammad (Sunnah).

**bismillah**  Reference to the phrase "Bismillah al-Rahman al-Rahim," meaning "In the name of God, the Merciful, the Compassionate." Opening verse of the Quran, which is used to begin letters, books, speeches, ceremonies, and official documents throughout the Muslim world.

**Black Muslim**   Adherent of African-American strain of Islam, member of African-American sect Nation of Islam.

**burqa**   Full veil covering a woman, which leaves only the eyes visible, worn by women in Afghanistan under Taliban regime.

**caliph**   Title for successor to Muhammad as political leader of Muslim community.

**chador**   Iranian term for woman's veil that covers hair and body, leaving only face, hands and feet exposed.

**Constitution of Medina**   Constitution promulgated by Muhammad, which established principle of religious pluralism within single political entity.

**dar al-Islam**   "Abode of peace." Muslim territories; territories ruled by Islamic law.

**dawa**   Literally, "call." Missionary work.

**dhimmi**   Person enjoying protected status due to treaty relationship with Muslims. Typically used to refer to "People of the Book," particularly Jews and Christians.

**din, deen.**   Religion.

**dua**   Invocation. Private prayer of petition.

**Eid al-Adha**   Feast of the Sacrifice. Major Muslim holiday falling at the end of the pilgrimage to Mecca *(hajj)*.

**Eid al-Fitr**   Feast of the Breaking of the Fast. Major Muslim holiday that concludes the month of Ramadan, during which Muslims fast.

**Fatima**   Daughter of Muhammad, wife of Ali, and mother of Hassan and Hussein. Example of perfect womanhood in Islam.

**fatwa**   Legal opinion issued by a private religious scholar (as opposed to a judge in a court of law). May be used by a judge in rendering a legal ruling.

**fez**   Red cap traditionally worn by Turkish men prior to the twentieth century.

**Five Pillars of Islam**   The five acts required of all Muslims: profession of faith, prayer five times daily, almsgiving *(zakat)*, fasting during Ramadan, and *hajj* (pilgrimage) once in a lifetime.

**hadith** Traditions, reports of Muhammad's deeds and sayings, considered to be a source of scripture for Muslims.

**hajj** Pilgrimage to Mecca, which Muslims are required to make at least once in a lifetime if they are physically and financially able. One of the Five Pillars of Islam.

**halal** Meat that has been prepared in a ritually appropriate way.

**Hanafi** Major Sunni Islamic law school. Predominates in the Arab world and South Asia.

**Hanbali** Major Sunni Islamic law school. Predominates in Saudi Arabia.

**Hidden Imam** Shii belief that the twelfth Imam did not die but went into hiding or "occultation," from which he is expected to return at the end of time as a messianic figure to bring in an era of peace and justice.

**hijab** Veil covering the hair and head of a Muslim woman. Can include long-sleeved, long, flowing dress as well.

**hijra** Emigration. Refers to departure of Muhammad and early Muslims from Mecca for Medina, which marks first year of Muslim lunar calendar.

**hudud** Literally, "limits." Refers to crimes of theft, extramarital sexual activity, false accusations of unchastity, and consumption of alcohol specified by the Quran and carrying harsh capital penalties.

**Hussein** Grandson of Muhammad and son of Ali and Fatima. Massacred in Karbala, Iraq, along with followers when he tried to claim sovereignty over Muslim community in 680 C.E. Massacre set paradigm of suffering, oppression, and need to fight injustice for Shii Muslims.

**ijma** Consensus.

**ijtihad** Independent reasoning in interpretation of Islamic law.

**imam** Prayer leader and person who delivers Friday sermon for Sunni Muslims. Shii Muslims use Imam as title for Muhammad's male descendants through Ali and Fatima. Shiis believe that Imams, although human, were divinely inspired and infallible, rendering their writings and legal interpretations additional sources of scripture.

**intifada**   Palestinian uprising that began in 1987. So-called second intifada began in 2000.

**Islam**   Literally, "submission."

**Ismaili**   "Sevener" branch of Shii Islam, which recognizes seven Imams. Founders of Fatimid Empire.

**istihsan**   Equity; using personal judgment to mitigate literal application of law.

**Ithna Ashari**   "Twelver" branch of Shii Islam, which recognizes twelve Imams, the last of whom is believed to be in hiding (see "Hidden Imam"). Majority of Shiis belong to this branch.

**Jafari**   Major Shii school of Islamic law.

**jihad**   Literally, "struggle" or "exertion." "Greater" jihad is the struggle within oneself to live a righteous life and submit oneself to God's will. "Lesser" jihad is the defense of Islam and the Muslim community.

**jizya**   Poll or head tax paid by *dhimmis* in order to enter into protective treaty relationship with Muslims.

**juma**   Friday congregational prayer.

**Kaaba**   Muslim House of God. Cube containing the Black Stone, which Muslims believe was given to Abraham by the angel Gabriel and placed in the Kaaba by Abraham and Ismail. Located in Mecca. Focal point of the *hajj*.

**kafir**   Unbeliever.

**keffiyah**   Traditional male head covering typically associated with Palestine and Jordan.

**Khadija**   Muhammad's first and only wife for twenty-four years, the first convert to and one of the strongest supporters of Islam.

**Kharijites**   Extremist minority sect of Muslims who broke with the early Muslim community over Ali's willingness to compromise in conflict, which they interpreted as a failure to act within God's will. Ultimately assassinated Ali due to their belief that he had committed apostasy. Believed that the world was strictly divided into two spheres, the realm of Islam and the realm of unbelief, so that only two categories of people were possible: believers or unbelievers, who were, by definition, enemies of Muslims. Inspired contemporary movements like Islamic Jihad and al-Qaeda.

**khutba**  Sermon preached during Friday congregational prayer.

**Mahdi**  Muslim messianic figure expected to return at the end of time to usher in an era of peace and justice.

**Maliki**  Major Sunni Islamic law school. Predominant in North, Central, and West Africa.

**mamluk**  Slave soldier. Became part of social and political elite under Muslim dynasties.

**masjid**  Mosque, place for Muslim prayer.

**maslaha**  Public interest or public welfare. Concept that allows for consideration of public interest in interpreting Islamic law.

**Mecca**  Holiest city in Islam. Birthplace of Muhammad and location of the Kaaba. City where Muslims go on the *hajj*. Located in Saudi Arabia.

**Medina**  Second holiest city in Islam. City to which Muhammad and the early Muslims emigrated (*hijra*) when they were forced to leave Mecca. City where Muhammad is buried. Located in Saudi Arabia.

**mihrab**  Niche in mosque wall indicating direction of Mecca, toward which all Muslims must pray.

**millet**  Religious or faith community officially recognized by the Ottoman Empire.

**minaret**  High tower in a mosque from which the call to prayer (*adhan*) is made.

**minbar**  Pulpit in a mosque from which the Friday sermon (*kutba*) is delivered.

**mosque**  Muslim house of worship, where all Muslim men are required to attend Friday prayer services.

**mudarabah**  Islamic financial principle of profit-sharing, which abides by Islamic prohibition of usury.

**muezzin**  Person who issues the call to prayer (*adhan*).

**mufti**  Specialist in Islamic law who is capable of delivering a legal opinion (*fatwa*).

**Muhammad**  Prophet of Islam who received revelation of the Quran. Muslims believe that he was the perfect human being and seek to emulate his example (*Sunnah*), as recorded in the *hadith*.

**mujahid (pl., mujahidin)** Soldier of God.

**mujtahid** Person qualified to exercise independent reasoning (*ijtihad*) in the interpretation of Islamic law.

**musharakah** Islamic financial principle of equity-sharing, which abides by Islamic prohibition of usury.

**Muslim** Literally, "one who submits." Adherent of faith of Islam.

**Muwahhidun** Literally, "Unitarians," or upholders of absolute monotheism. Also called Wahhabis.

**Nation of Islam** African-American strain of Islam that initially preached message of black supremacy, militancy, and separatism but has become more in line with mainstream Sunni Islam since the late 1990s.

**Nizari Ismaili** Sect of "Sevener" Shiis. Historically known as Assassins. Contemporary movement is nonviolent. Leader today is known as Agha Khan.

**People of the Book** Religious group with a revealed scripture or divine revelation. Used by Muslims to refer to Christians and Jews.

**pir** Sufi master.

**qadi** Muslim judge.

**qibla** Direction of Mecca as indicated by niche (*mihrab*) in wall of mosque.

**qiyas** Islamic legal principle of analogical reasoning.

**Quran** Literally, "recitation." Muslim scripture or holy book revealed to Muhammad.

**raka** Muslim prayer unit.

**Ramadan** Muslim month of fasting, which ends with celebration of Eid al-Fitr. Fasting during Ramadan is one of the Five Pillars of Islam.

**riba** Usury or interest. Outlawed by Islamic law.

**salam** Peace.

**As-salam alaykum** Literally, "Peace be upon you." Muslim greeting. Response is "And peace be upon you also" or "Wa-alaykum as-salam."

**salat** Prayer. Required of all Muslims five times daily. One of the Five Pillars of Islam.

**sayyid** Descendant of Muhammad.

**Shafii** Major Sunni Islamic law school. Predominant in East Africa and Southeast Asia.

**shahada** Witness or testimony. Declaration "There is no god but God, and Muhammad is His messenger." One of the Five Pillars of Islam.

**shahid** Martyr.

**Shariah** Islamic law as established in the Quran and *hadith*.

**Shii** Muslims who believe that succession to the political and religious leadership of the Muslim community should be hereditary through Muhammad's daughter Fatima and her husband, Muhammad's cousin Ali. Although Shiis do not believe that these successors (Imams) are prophets, they do believe that they are divinely inspired and infallible. About 15 percent of all Muslims are Shiis.

**shura** Consultation.

**Sufi** Muslim mystic.

**Sunnah** Muhammad's example as recorded in the *hadith*.

**Sunni** Muslims who believe that succession to the political leadership of the Muslim community should belong to the most qualified and pious person, not be hereditary. They believe that the successor is strictly a political leader and a protector of the faith, not someone who is divinely inspired. About 85 percent of all Muslims are Sunnis.

**surah** Chapter of the Quran.

**takfir** Excommunication, exclusion for unbelief.

**taqlid** Unquestioned imitation or following of tradition, past legal or doctrinal precedents; the opposite of *ijtihad*.

**tawhid** Monotheism.

**tazir** Crimes punished at the discretion of a Muslim judge (*qadi*).

**turban** Head covering worn by some Muslim males, particularly in Afghanistan under the Taliban and in Iran.

**ulama**  Muslim religious scholars.

**ummah**  The worldwide Muslim community, community of believers.

**umrah**  Lesser pilgrimage in which Muslims visit Muhammad's tomb in Medina; visitation of Muslim holy sites outside of the *hajj*.

**Wahhabi**  Adherent of ultraconservative interpretation of Islam as practiced in Saudi Arabia.

**wali**  Literally, "friend," "helper," or "patron." Muslim saint.

**waqf**  Muslim religious endowment whose profits are used for charitable purposes.

**zakat**  Literally, "purification." Almsgiving or charitable giving consisting of 2.5 percent of a Muslim's entire wealth (not just income). One of the Five Pillars of Islam.

**Zamzam**  Literally, "bubbling." Well in Mecca that Muslims believe was revealed to Hagar by God in order to preserve her and Ismail from dying of thirst. Drinking water from this well is one of the *hajj* rituals.

**Zaydi**  Sect of Shii Islam also known as "Fivers" due to recognition of five Imams. Predominant in Yemen.

# SUGGESTIONS FOR FURTHER READING

## General Reference

Esposito, John L., editor-in-chief. *The Oxford Dictionary of Islam.* New York: Oxford University Press, 2002.

———, editor-in-chief. *The Oxford Encyclopedia of the Modern Islamic World.* 4 vols. New York: Oxford University Press, 1995.

———, ed. *The Oxford History of Islam.* New York: Oxford University Press, 1999.

Hodgson, Marshall G. S. *The Venture of Islam: Conscience and History in a World Civilization.* 3 vols. Chicago and London: University of Chicago Press, 1974.

Lapidus, Ira M. *A History of Islamic Societies.* Cambridge: Cambridge University Press, 1988.

Voll, John O. *Islam: Continuity and Change in the Modern World.* 2d ed. Syracuse: Syracuse University Press, 1994.

## Faith and Practice

Ali, A. Yusuf. *The Koran: Text, Translation, and Commentary.* Washington, D.C.: American International Printing Company, 1946.

*Al-Qu'ran: A Contemporary Translation.* Trans. Admed Ali. Princeton: Princeton University Press, 1988.

Armstrong, Karen. *Muhammad: A Biography of the Prophet.* San Francisco: HarperCollins, 1993.

Asad, Muhammad. *The Message of the Quran.* Gibraltar: Dar al-Andalus, 1980.

Chittick, William C. *The Sufi Path of Love: The Spiritual Teachings of Rumi.* Albany: State University of New York Press, 1984.

Esposito, John L. *Islam: The Straight Path.* 3d ed. New York: Oxford University Press, 1998.

Esposito, John L., and John O. Voll. *Makers of Contemporary Islam.* New York: Oxford University Press, 2001.

Fakhry, Majid, trans. *The Quran: A Modern English Version*. Berkshire: Garnet Publishing, 1996.

Guillaume, A., trans. and ed. *The Life of Muhammad: A Translation of Ibn Ishaq's* Sirat Rasul Allah. New York: Oxford University Press, 1997.

Haneef, Suzanne. *What Everyone Should Know About Islam and Muslims*. 12th ed. Chicago: Kazi Publications, 1995.

Lings, Martin. *Muhammad: His Life Based on the Earliest Sources*. London: Inner Traditions International, 1983.

———. *What Is Sufism?* Berkeley: University of California Press, 1977.

Momen, Moojan. *An Introduction to Shii Islam: The History and Doctrines of Twelver Shiism*. New Haven and London: Yale University Press, 1985.

Nasr, Seyyid Vali Reza. *Mawdudi and the Making of Islamic Revivalism*. New York: Oxford University Press, 1996.

Peters, F. E. *Muhammad and the Origins of Islam*. Albany: State University of New York Press, 1994.

Pickthall, Mohammed Marmaduke. *The Meaning of the Glorious Koran*. New York: New American Library and Mentor Books, n.d.

Rahman, Fazlur. *Islam*. Chicago: University of Chicago Press, 1979.

———. *Major Themes of the Qur'an*. Minneapolis and Chicago: Bibliotheca Islamica, 1980.

Rahnema, Ali. *An Islamic Utopian: A Political Biography of Ali Shari'ati*. New York: I. B. Tauris, 2000.

Renard, John. *Seven Doors to Islam: Spirituality and the Religious Life of Muslims*. Berkeley: University of California Press, 1996.

Sachedina, Abdulaziz. *The Islamic Roots of Democratic Pluralism*. New York: Oxford University Press, 2001.

Sadri, Mahmoud, and Ahmad Sadri, trans. and eds. *Reason, Freedom, and Democracy in Islam: Essential Writings of Abdolkarim Soroush*. New York: Oxford University Press, 2000.

Sardar, Ziauddin, and Zafar Abbas Malik. *Muhammad for Beginners*. New York: Totem Books, 1994.

Schimmel, Annemarie. *And Muhammad Is His Messenger: The Veneration of the Prophet in Islamic Piety*. Chapel Hill and London: University of North Carolina Press, 1985.

———. *Mystical Dimensions of Islam*. Chapel Hill and London: University of North Carolina Press, 1975.

Sedgwick, Mark J. *Sufism: The Essentials*. Cairo: The American University in Cairo Press, 2000.

Tamimi, Azzam S. *Rachid Ghannouchi: A Democrat Within Islamism*. New York: Oxford University Press, 2001.

Trimingham, J. Spencer. *The Sufi Orders in Islam*. New York: Oxford University Press, 1998.

Wadud, Amina. *Qur'an and Woman: Rereading the Sacred Text from a Woman's Perspective*. New York: Oxford University Press, 1999.

Watt, W. Montgomery. *Muhammad: Prophet and Statesman*. New York: Oxford University Press, 1960.

Wolfe, Michael. *The Hadj: An American's Pilgrimage to Mecca*. New York: Grove Press, 1998.

————, ed. *One Thousand Roads to Mecca : Ten Centuries of Travelers Writing About the Muslim Pilgrimage*. New York: Grove Press, 1999.

## Islam and Other Religions

Armstrong, Karen. *The Battle for God: Fundamentalism in Judaism, Christianity, and Islam*. London and New York: Alfred A. Knopf, 2000.

————. *Holy War: The Crusades and Their Impact on Today's World*. New York: Doubleday, 1991.

Haddad, Yvonne Yazbeck, and Wadi Z. Haddad. *Christian-Muslim Encounters*. Gainesville: University Press of Florida, 1995.

Lewis, Bernard. *The Jews of Islam*. Princeton: Princeton University Press, 1984.

Menocal, Maria Rosa, and Harold Bloom. *The Ornament of the World: How Muslims, Jews, and Christians Created a Culture of Tolerance in Medieval Spain*. New York: Little, Brown, 2002.

Peters, F. E. *Children of Abraham*. Princeton: Princeton University Press, 1982.

Watt, W. Montgomery. *Islam and Christianity Today*. London: Routledge and Kegan Paul, 1983.

## Customs and Culture

Abou El Fadl, Khaled, et al. *Speaking in God's Name: Islamic Law, Authority and Women*. Oxford: One World Publications, 2001.

Ahmed, Leila. *Women and Gender in Islam: Historical Roots of a Modern Debate*. New Haven: Yale University Press, 1992.

Esposito, John L., with Natana J. De Long-Bas. *Women in Muslim Family Law*. 2d ed. Syracuse: Syracuse University Press, 2001.

Haddad, Yvonne Yazbeck, and John L. Esposito, eds. *Islam, Gender, and Social Change*. New York: Oxford University Press, 1998.

MacLeod, Arlene Elowe. *Accommodating Protest: Working Women, the New Veiling, and Change in Cairo*. New York: Columbia University Press, 1991.

Mernissi, Fatima. *The Veil and the Male Elite: A Feminist Interpretation of Women's Rights in Islam.* Trans. Mary Jo Lakeland. New York: Addison-Wesley, 1991.

Mir-Hosseini, Ziba. *Islam and Gender: The Religious Debate in Contemporary Iran.* Princeton: Princeton University Press, 1999.

Poya, Maryam. *Women, Work, and Islamism: Ideology and Resistance in Iran.* London: Zed Books, 1999.

## Violence and Terrorism

Esposito, John L. *The Islamic Threat: Myth or Reality?* 3d ed. New York: Oxford University Press, 1999.

———. *Unholy War: Terror in the Name of Islam.* New York: Oxford University Press, 2002.

Hroub, Khaled. *Hamas: Political Thought and Practice.* Washington, D.C.: Institute for Palestine Studies, 2000.

Jansen, Johannes J. G. *The Neglected Duty: The Creed of Sadat's Assassins and Islamic Resurgence in the Middle East.* New York and London: The Free Press, 1988.

Peters, Rudolph. *Jihad in Classical and Modern Islam.* Princeton: Markus Wiener Publishers, 1996.

Qutb, Sayyid. *Milestones.* Boll Ridge, Ind.: American Trust Publications, 1988.

———. *This Religion of Islam.* Chicago: Kazi Publications, 1996.

Rashid, Ahmed. *Taliban: Militant Islam, Oil, and Fundamentalism in Central Asia.* New Haven: Yale University Press, 2000.

Saad-Ghorayeb, Amal. *Hizbu'llah: Politics and Religion.* London: Pluto Press, 2002.

## Society, Politics, and Economy

Abdo, Geneive. *No God but God: Egypt and the Triumph of Islam.* New York: Oxford University Press, 2000.

Armstrong, Karen. *Jerusalem: One City, Three Faiths.* New York: Alfred A. Knopf, 1996.

Coulson, Noel J. *A History of Islamic Law.* Edinburgh: Edinburgh University Press, 1964.

Esposito, John L. *Islam and Politics.* 4th ed. Syracuse: Syracuse University Press, 1998.

Esposito, John L., and John O. Voll. *Islam and Democracy.* New York: Oxford University Press, 1996.

Hallaq, Wael. *A History of Islamic Legal Theories: An Introduction to Sunni usul al-fiqh.* Cambridge: Cambridge University Press, 1997.

Mills, Paul S., and John R. Presley. *Islamic Finance: Theory and Practice.* New York: St. Martin's Press, 1999.

Musallam, B. F. *Sex and Society in Islam.* Cambridge: Cambridge University Press, 1983.

Saeed, Abdullah. *Islamic Banking and Interest: A Study of the Prohibition of Riba and Its Contemporary Interpretation.* Leiden: E. J. Brill, 1996.

Vogel, Frank E., and Samuel L. Hayes III. *Islamic Law and Finance: Religion, Risk, and Return.* Boston: Kluwer Law International, 1998.

## Muslims in the West

Daniel, Norman. *Islam and the West: The Making of an Image.* Rev. ed. Oxford: One World, 1993.

Esposito, John L., Yvonne Haddad, and Jane Smith. *Immigrant Faiths: Christians, Jews, and Muslims Becoming Americans.* Walnut Creek, Calif.: Alta Mira Press, 2002.

Haddad, Yvonne Yazbeck, ed. *Muslims in the West: From Sojourners to Citizens.* New York: Oxford University Press, 2002.

Haddad, Yvonne Yazbeck, and John L. Esposito, eds. *Muslims on the Americanization Path.* Atlanta: Scholars Press, 1997.

Nielsen, Jorgen. *Muslims in Western Europe.* 2d ed. Edinburgh: Edinburgh University Press, 1995.

———. *Towards a European Islam.* London: St. Martin's Press, 1999.

Ramadas, Tariq. *To Be a European Muslim.* Leicester: The Islamic Foundation, 1998.

Said, Edward W. *Culture and Imperialism.* New York: Vintage Books, 1993.

———. *Covering Islam: How the Media and the Experts Determine How We See the Rest of the World.* New York: Pantheon Books, 1981.

# INDEX

Note: Page numbers in *italics* refer to glossary entries.